Suffolk Tow~ ~~ils

An easy to follow p

Michael And

Published by

Suffolk Country Walks

Text: Michael Anderton
Photographs: Michael Anderton
Maps: Sandra Canning

ISBN 0–9543425–0–X

Published by:
Suffolk Country Walks,
26 West Mill Green, Bentley, Ipswich
Suffolk IP9 2BN

Origination, typeset and printed in Great Britain by
Healeys Printers Ltd,
Unit 10, The Sterling Complex, Farthing Road, Ipswich,
Suffolk IP1 5AP

Front Cover: The Butter Cross, Bungay

Suffolk Town Trails

Preface

Between 1994 and 2001 I surveyed, photographed and produced weekly country walks for the Ipswich Evening Star newspaper, published on every Saturday of the six years, except for on two occasions. This rather daunting task was made comparatively easy for me really because my day job was working in Suffolk County Council's Public Rights of Way Department where I had access to information and publications that I could use for my walk articles. However, on some Saturday's I produced a town trail or a walk around a town park in order to broaden the scope of the series and to provide for people that did not want to walk in the countryside. Over this period of six years I built up a collection of these town trails which, as a result of the Foot and Mouth disease outbreak, were considerably added to during 2001. This book is therefore my collection of town trails, all based on the historic and picturesque market towns and administration centres of Suffolk.

Michael Anderton
Summer 2002

Disclaimer

The information in this book is given in good faith and is believed to be correct at the time of publication. No responsibility is accepted by either the author or publisher for errors or omissions, or for any loss or injury howsoever caused. Only you can judge your own fitness, competence and experience.

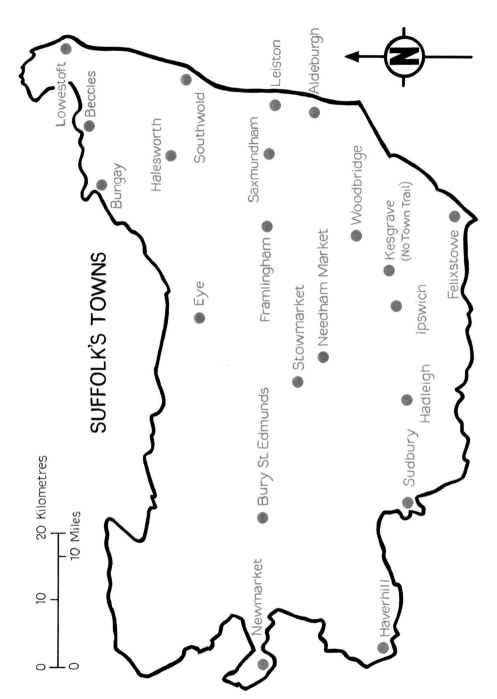

SUFFOLK'S TOWNS

Lowestoft
Beccles
Halesworth
Southwold
Leiston
Aldeburgh
Saxmundham
Bungay
Woodbridge
Kesgrave (No Town Trail)
Felixstowe
Eye
Framlingham
Needham Market
Stowmarket
Ipswich
Hadleigh
Bury St. Edmunds
Sudbury
Newmarket
Haverhill

20 Kilometres
10 Miles
10
0
0

Reproduced from Ordnance Survey mapping on behalf of The Controller of Her Majesty's Stationery Office © Crown Copyright. Licence Number AL100037826.

Suffolk Town Trails

The County of Suffolk

The ancient County of Suffolk was divided, by the Local Government Act of 1888, into East and West Suffolk with the respective administrative headquarters at Ipswich and Bury St. Edmunds. However, the county was reunited by the Local Government Act of 1974, with the headquarters of Suffolk County Council based in the county town of Ipswich. Suffolk is subdivided into seven Borough and District Councils and over 450 town and parish councils that serve the county at a local level.

Even so, the county is still divided naturally by the essentially different types of country that exist. On the east side is the coast with its numerous rivers and estuaries, forming large stretches of marshland, interspersed here and there with patches of sandy heath and moorland. This part of the county is characterised by its fine woodlands, and the rich fertile soil that borders the many waterways. The west side of the county, though slightly more hilly, rises nowhere to any great height. It is not so diversified with trees as is the eastern side of the county, but in its southern part it is exceedingly good agricultural land and produces first-class crops. Its northern part consists largely of a more desolate and wild patch of moorland, known as Breckland or The Brecks, which extends into the adjoining county of Norfolk.

Towns

There are many large villages and small towns in Suffolk and it is difficult to draw the line between town and village when it comes to making up a short list such as is produced here. In order to avoid any argument over what should or should not be included in this book, the definition of a town has been taken to be a community that is administered by a town council. This has unfortunately excluded places like Brandon, Debenham, Lavenham, Mildenhall and Orford, all of which are administered by parish councils. But a line had to be drawn somewhere and perhaps there is scope for another book featuring the parish trails of the larger villages of the county. There are 21 recorded town councils in Suffolk, all of them ancient towns with the exception of Kesgrave, which only became a town on 1 January 2000. It is for this reason that Kesgrave is not included in this book that features the remaining 20 ancient towns of Suffolk.

Town Trails

This collection of town trails has been developed from a number of sources, mainly of which are the many leaflets and booklets that can be obtained from local Tourist Information Centres, libraries and book shops etc. Therefore much of this work has already been published in some form or other and acknowledgement of the sources is included with each of the town trail Fact Files where relevant. Some of the trails have been developed from information supplied by local history groups and other enthusiasts who are keen to see their local community publicised in this way. In some cases a draft or out of print trail leaflet has been supplied from which a trail to fit this publication has been produced. Whatever the case, the origin of the information has been acknowledged, without these sources the book could not have been produced. Of course, many of the town trail publications give much more detail than is provided here, but each of these trails will give you an insight to the history and layout of the towns that are featured. It is highly recommended that the reader seek out these original publications where available and also the local contacts if further reading or other aspects about the town and its history are required.

Place names

Suffolk's towns have fascinating names that can usually be interpreted to find their origins and meanings. Where information is given about place names in the trail descriptions, it has generally been taken from 'A Popular Guide to Suffolk Place Names' by James Rye. (Published by The Larks Press – ISBN 0948400552 – price £3.95). This little booklet is most useful to historians and writers in determining how the names originated, the descriptions often point to why a particular settlement evolved in that location, of the people who first inhabited area or of the wildlife that they found.

What to wear

Most of the trails in this book will only require comfortable walking shoes and normal townwear to explore the routes that are described. However, it should be remembered that some routes are up to 3 miles long, sometimes using unsurfaced paths, and may be a little exposed if the weather turns inclement. If rain is imminent it would be prudent to carry a waterproof or umbrella and, where the paths are likely to be muddy (see Fact File information with each trail), waterproof footwear should be worn.

Public Transport

These days the public transport system is in constant change and services come and go overnight. Details of Suffolk County Council's excellent public transport information service are provided with each of the trail Fact Files. By telephoning the TraveLine on 08459 583358 at local call rate from anywhere, up to date details about bus, coach and rail journeys in Suffolk can be obtained. When you call you should have a pen and paper to record the answers and the following information ready about your journey:–

- Where you want to travel from
- Where you want to travel to
- The time and date you want to travel
- If you want to break your journey

The TraveLine is open:–

- Monday to Friday 0845 to 1800
- Saturday 0900 to 1230
- Answerphone at all other times or by visiting their website at http://www.traveline.suffolkcc.gov.uk

Local rail information can be obtained by telephoning Anglia Rail on 08700 402020 or by visiting their website at http://www.angliarailways.co.uk/

Tourist Information Centres

Aldeburgh Tourist Information Centre, 152 High Street, IP15 5AU – tel. 01728 453637

Beccles Broads Information Centre, The Quay, Fen Lane, NR34 9BH – tel. 0150 2713196

Brandon Tourist Information Centre, 31 High Street – tel. 01842 814955

Bury St. Edmunds Tourist Information Centre, Angel Hill, IP33 IUZ – tel. 01284 764667

Flatford Visitor Information Centre, Flatford Lane, East Bergholt, CO7 6UL – tel. 01206 299460

Felixstowe Tourist Information Centre, Leisure Centre, Sea Front, IP11 8AE – tel. 01394 276770

Ipswich Tourist Information Centre, St. Stephen's Church, St. Stephen's Lane, IP1 1DP – tel. 01473 258070

Lavenham Tourist Information Centre, Lady Street, C010 9RA – tel. 01787 248207

Lowestoft Tourist Information Centre, The East Point Pavilion, Royal Plain NR33 0AP – tel. 01502 533600

Newmarket Tourist Information Centre, Palace House, Palace Street, CB8 8EP – tel. 01638 667200

Southwold Tourist Information Centre, High Street, IP18 6EG – tel. 01502 724729

Stowmarket, Mid Suffolk Tourist Information Centre, Wilkes Way, IP14 1DE – tel. 01449 676800

Sudbury Tourist Information Centre, Town Hall, Market Hill, CO10 1TL – tel. 01787 881320

Woodbridge Tourist Information Centre, Station Buildings, Station Road IP12 4AJ – tel. 01394 382240

Bibliography

The County of Suffolk Official Guide – circa 1950

Suffolk, a Shire County Guide – Tim Buxbaum

The Suffolk Village Book – Suffolk Federation of Women's Institutes

A Popular Guide to Place Names – James Rye

East Anglia's First Railways – Hugh Moffat

The East Suffolk Railway – Rosemary Burton

LNER Branch Lines – C. J. Gammell

Contents

Moot Hall

Martello Tower

1. Aldeburgh

Until 1800 Aldeburgh had been prominent as a maritime and fishing centre but these pursuits declined as shipbuilding moved away and the larger fishing boats became difficult to winch up the beach. In the 19th century new residents and holiday makers moved in, building houses on the outer edges of the town and encouraged activities such as walking, sailing, bathing and golf. Although 6 streets of the old town have been lost to the sea since the 16th century, this trail explores what remains, guarded from the North Sea by modern sea defences.

The walk starts from the Moot Hall (1), dating from about 1540, it contains a museum largely devoted to the town's history and the chambers of the Town Council. Walk north into Market Cross Place with the White Lion Hotel (2) on the left, the beach and fisherman's huts on the right and ahead, views up the coast of Sizewell Power Station and the House in the Clouds at Thorpeness. Turn left at the end of the White Lion Hotel to reach Wentworth Road, then left along the rear of the hotel and right up Victoria Road, also known as Church Hill.

The Parish Church of Saints Peter and Paul (3) stands above the town on the cliffs and dates partly from the 14th century with an unusual porch extending to the road. It was extended and improved in the 16th century and contains a memorial to Aldeburgh's poet George Crabbe, in the churchyard are the graves of Benjamin Britten and Peter Pears.

Continue on to Uplands Hotel (4) on the left, home of Elizabeth Garrett Anderson, the country's first female doctor and surgeon and also the birthplace of Millicent Garrett Fawcett, leader of the Suffragette Movement. Follow the road past the County Library at Triangle Wood (5) and on to the roundabout ahead (200 metres). All that remains of Aldeburgh's railway station complex is the Railway Inn, the station once stood to right of the pub, the site is now built on and nothing remains. The branch line closed in 1966 and once brought holidaymakers on excursion trains from London via Ipswich and the junction with the East Coast Line at Saxmundham.

Return back along Victoria Road to Triangle Wood (5) and turn right by the town sign along Park Road. This area between the cliffs and marshes is known as Garrett Aldeburgh and was developed in the late 19th century by Newson Garrett who also developed Snape Maltings. He included an improved water supply and sewage disposal system in his plans and his water tower (6), now unused, can be seen behind the trees at the next junction. Turn right along Priors Hill Road with the water tower on the left.

Follow the curving road around, passing several more large houses with extensive gardens, until you reach Park Road. Turn left up the hill past Cherry House (7), a large pink house on the right once owned by Russian cellist Rostropovich, and then on the left, Aldebugh's Community Hospital (8). Turn right on Park Lane, a stony track, passing between the posts forming a barrier to continue on the lane towards the town. Just before crossing Alde Lane note Alde House (9) behind the trees on the left, built by Newson Garrett as a family home.

Continue straight on to reach the top of the Town Steps at the junction with Church Walk. Across the road stands the Roman Catholic Church (10), built in flint in the 1930s, it lost its tower in 1945. Part way down the Town Steps is the town pump and at the bottom on the right, a row of Fisherman's Cottages (11). Cross the High Street and Crabbe Street then through Oakley Square to reach Crag Path on the sea front.

Turn right past the first (12) of two lookout towers, once used by rival fishing and piloting groups and providing an unusual feature to the skyline. Walk south along Crag Path and, just before the second (13) lookout tower, note the group of houses (14) that add to the variety of architecture, including Fantasia, a former barber's shop, North Gable and Strafford House.

Continue on past the Brundenell Hotel (15) to reach the car park at Fort Green (16). Turn left around the Old Mill (17), a former windmill that once ground flour for the town. At the time of the Romans the River Alde entered the sea here but the shifting coastline has left it as a vulnerable point during times of flood. Follow the sea wall south towards the Martello Tower (1000 metres), past Slaughden Yacht Club, all that remains of a community lost to the sea in the 1920s. During the 17th century it had 3 quays, employed 600 people and was the business centre of Aldeburgh.

Continue on past the Aldeburgh Yacht Club to reach the Martello Tower. Built in 1815 of yellow-pink Thames brick, it was the largest and most northerly of a chain of 102 such fortifications stretching down to Hampshire. Return along the sea wall to Fort Green (16), continuing straight on along the wide High Street.

Look out on the left for a fine group of houses (18) that includes No. 227, a timber framed house and Old Custom House (19) with its stone steps leading to the front door, all reputedly built directly onto the shingle. As you continue on up the High Street you will find the Tourist Information Centre (20) on the right, next door to The Suffolk (21), formerly a hotel and now the headquarters and booking office of the Aldeburgh Foundation. Opposite is the Baptist Chapel (22) of 1822, still used for worship and also small concerts.

At the widest part of the High Street stands Baggott's Corner (23), on the left is the new Post Office (24) replacing one bombed in 1942. Take the right fork along Crabbe Street, passing Oakley Square, the rear of the 16th century Cross Keys Inn (25) and Jubilee Hall (26), enlarged by Newson Garret for Queen Victoria's Jubilee and used for a variety of events, notably the Aldeburgh Festival. Finally walk past No. 4 (27) where Benjamin Britten lived until 1957, to return to the start of the walk at the Moot Hall (1).

Fact File

Location: Aldeburgh is 25 miles north east of Ipswich
Start: Moot Hall, Crabbe Street, Ordnance Survey map reference TM 465568
Length: 3 miles
Conditions: Road and roadside footway, river wall shingle path
How to get there:–
Public Transport: For details telephone Suffolk County Council's Public Transport Information Service – 08459 583358
By Road: From Ipswich on A1214 and A12 north, before Saxmundham follow A1094 to Aldeburgh
Car parking: Pay and display at Fort Green and other sites (some free) in the town
Refreshments: The town supports a wide range of facilities such pubs, restaurants and shops
Public Toilets: Moot Hall, Fort Green and High Street
Map: Ordnance Survey Explorer sheet 212 Woodbridge & Saxmundham
Reference: Around Aldeburgh by the Aldeburgh Society and the Suffolk Preservation Society
Information: Aldeburgh Tourist Information Centre – open daily

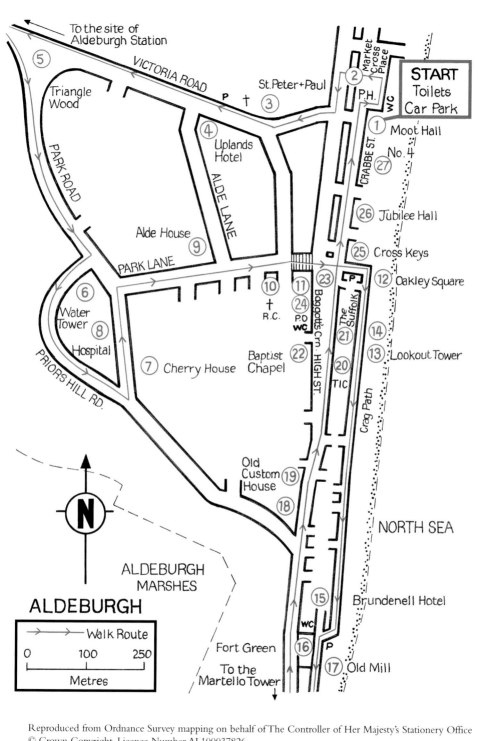

To the site of
Aldeburgh Station

⑤

Triangle
Wood

VICTORIA ROAD

Market
Cross
Place

② P.H.

START
Toilets
Car Park

WC

St.Peter+Paul

P †

③

① Moot Hall

PARK ROAD

④

Uplands
Hotel

ALDE LANE

CRABBE ST.

No.4

㉗

⑥

Alde House

⑨

PARK LANE

⑩ ⑪ ㉓

† R.C.

㉔

P.O

WC

Baggott's Crn. HIGH ST.

㉖ Jubilee Hall

㉕ Cross Keys

P

⑫ Oakley Square

The Suffolk

⑭

⑬ Lookout Tower

Water
Tower

⑧

Hospital

⑦ Cherry House

PRIORS HILL RD.

Baptist
Chapel

㉒

㉑

⑳

TIC

Crag Path

Old
Custom
House

⑲

⑱

N

NORTH SEA

ALDEBURGH
MARSHES

ALDEBURGH

⑮ Brundenell Hotel

WC

⑯

P

Fort Green

To the
Martello Tower

⑰ Old Mill

Walk Route

0   100   250

Metres

Town Sign

Quaker Meeting House

Leman House Museum

2. Beccles

The origin of Beccles can be found in the name which means 'pasture by a stream', and standing on the edge of a cliff, the position was ideal for the early settlers. The area would originally have been mainly marsh but over the centuries the marshland gradually decreased and was drained and ditched under the control of the Abbotts of St. Edmundsbury. With a fine bridge across the river and access to the sea, the port of Beccles had a transport system to move goods for trade. The economy expanded even further with the advent of the railways and the river gradually became the thriving holiday industry that we see today.

From The Quay walk up Fen Lane past the old warehouses and other buildings that have been converted for modern use, no longer required for the trade that once arrived via the river. At Bridge Street turn right to Beccles Bridge (1), built in 1884 to replace a 15th century stone structure. The bridge gave Beccles considerable prosperity in mediaeval times and today provides a fine river view of the town.

Return to the crossroads and turn right up Northgate, one of the most attractive streets in the town and containing several notable houses. Of particular note are Tannery House (2) where the local tannery once stood, Montague House (3), the home of Captain Edward Montague RN JP from 1823 to 1860 and Oswald House (4) with a Dutch gable end, the home of a 19th century tanner. Adrian Bell, writer and father of Martin Bell the former war correspondent, lived at No. 19 (5) from 1954 from 1964, formerly the home of a 18th century glove and breeches maker. Just before the end of the street note The Score (6), a public access where goods could be loaded and unloaded at the river.

Walk up through the Old Market Place, probably the original Anglo Saxon site of Fairs and Markets, and into Saltgate where at No. 5 (7) Chateaubriand, a French aristocrat and writer stayed as a haven from the French Revolution and taught in a local school in 1794. Just before reaching the Church of St. Michael turn right on the path through the churchyard and along the cliff top path at the rear. Below stands the Waveney House Hotel (8), with 16th or 17th century flint walls, it was probably thatched at one time.

Turn left at the corner by the steps and head towards the Church Tower. St. Michael's Church (9) was built between 1350 and 1400, with the south porch added in 1450, and is built within 24 acres that were mentioned in Domesday. The church suffered badly in the Great Fire of Beccles of 1586, the interior was destroyed and damage to the town amounted to £20,000. It was here in 1749 that Catherine Suckling married the Reverend Edward Nelson and later gave birth to Lord Horatio Nelson, one of the greatest seafarers known. A guidebook describing the church is well worth obtaining if you are entering and is available within for £1.50.

Work on building the bell tower commenced in 1500, it weighs about 3000 tons and took 40 years to complete. It is uniquely situated to the east of the church and was positioned there because it was not safe to build to the west on the cliffside. There is a peal of ten bells in the belfry, weighing six tons and originally installed in 1762, later restored and rehung in 1909.

Walk around the front of the red brick octagonal shaped Town Hall (10), built in 1765 and standing on the site of the original medieval Market Cross. Turn right in Newmarket, developed in the 13th century by the Abbot of Bury to cater for the growing trade, walking around the block of quaint little shops that stand on the original 17th century wooden stalls. Note the narrow passages between the buildings, in 1659 there were 51 stalls here. At the back of Newmarket stands the White Horse pub (11), the entrance to the yard was the access to the coach house and stables.

Turn left along Balleygate, another fine street with 18th century facades and panoramic views across the river, passing Stepping Hill (12) on the right, a set of steps down to Puddingmoor below. The Beccles Museum is housed in Leman House (13), a Grade 1 listed building that was given to the town by John Leman, once Lord Mayor of London, in his will of 1631. It was a Free School for boys and originally thatched.

At the end of the road stands the town sign (14) depicting Queen Elizabeth I presenting the Beccles Charter to Edward Baas in 1584. Turn left to view St. Benet's Roman Catholic Church (15), built between 1890 and 1910 and designed by local architect Francis Easto Banham. Return to the town sign and along Ballygate, turning right into Hungate Lane, past an 18th century crinkle crankle wall (16), and on into Hungate. Turn left through Exchange Square and on along Smallgate where a number of interesting buildings can be seen.

On the right is the Quaker Meeting House (17) set back behind Quaker House, Tilney's Gunsmith, owned and run by the same family since 1860 and the Public Hall (18), built in 1786 and used as an assembly room, theatre and for balls and feasts. On the left stands the splendid Co-operative Store (19), designed by Beccles architect Arthur Pells, the modest southern part dates from 1898 while the city style northern end dates from 1913. Opposite is the former Primitive Methodist Chapel (20) built in 1871 and now occupied by Taylor Electrical.

At Old Market follow the road around to the right to view Ravensmere House (21) with a fine Dutch Gable end. Displayed is the date of 1694 when it was owned by a malster, Abraham Browne whose family lived there for the next 100 years. Return to Old Market and walk through to Northgate, turning right to return to the start of the trail at the Quay.

Fact File

Location: Beccles is 40 miles north of Ipswich and 19 miles south east of Norwich
Start: Broads Authority Information Centre, Ordnance Survey map reference TM 421911
Length: 2 miles
Conditions: Road and roadside footway throughout

How to get there:–
Public Transport: For details telephone Suffolk County Council's Public Transport Information TraveLine – 08459 583358 or Anglia Rail – 08700 402020
By Road: From Ipswich on A12 and A145 or from Norwich on A146
Car Parking: Free at Fen Lane car park, other parking also available in the town
Refreshments: A wide range of pubs, shops and restaurants available in the town
Public Toilets: The Quay and Sheepgate
Map: Ordnance Survey Outdoor Leisure sheet 40 – The Broads
Reference: Beccles Revealed by David Lindley and the Beccles Society, and Beccles Town Guide by the Beccles Town Council
Information: Beccles Broads Information Centre, open daily Easter to October

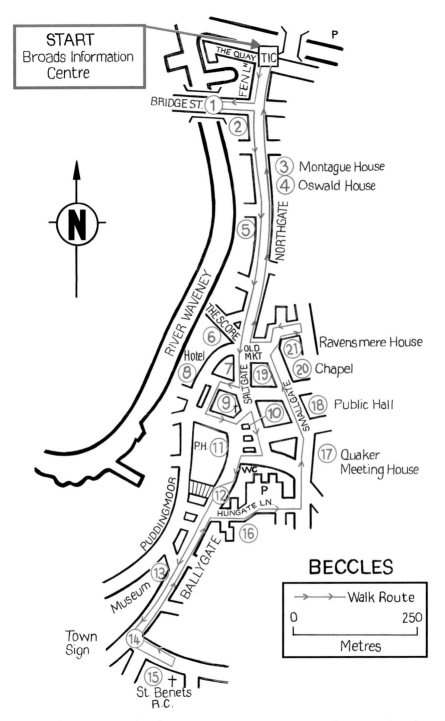

START
Broads Information
Centre

BRIDGE ST. ①
②
③ Montague House
④ Oswald House
⑤
⑥
Hotel
⑧   ⑦
⑨
⑩
P.H. ⑪
⑫
⑬
⑭
⑮
St. Benets
R.C.
Town
Sign

RIVER WAVENEY
THE QUAY
FEN LN
TIC
P
NORTHGATE
THE SCORE
OLD MKT
SALTGATE
SMALLGATE
WC
P
HUNGATE LN.
⑯
⑰ Quaker
Meeting House
⑱ Public Hall
⑲
⑳ Chapel
㉑
Ravensmere House
PUDDINGMOOR
BALLYGATE
Museum

BECCLES

→→ Walk Route

0   250

Metres

N

Reproduced from Ordnance Survey mapping on behalf of The Controller of Her Majesty's Stationery Office
© Crown Copyright. Licence Number AL100037826.

Bungay Castle

St. Mary's Church

3. Bungay

Bungay is practically surrounded by a loop of the River Waveney and this is reflected in the Old English meaning of the town's name, Bunahea, the island belonging to Buna's people. The ancient market town is built around a Norman fortress, once the stronghold of the Bigods, and much remains for the visitor to explore, including the castle keep. The river afforded trading access to the sea until 1934 and the local oak woods provided suitable timber used to build the famous wherries that once worked the navigation.

The Bungay Town Trail consists of two loops, east and west, marked with red and yellow triangles, and starts at the famous Butter Cross in the centre of the town. This was built after the Great Fire of 1688 and in earlier times was used as a prison with dungeon below, on the top of the dome shaped roof is the figure of Justice holding the traditional scales and sword. The Butter Cross is now only a place to rest and is used as a shelter for the market stalls every Thursday.

For the eastern route, walk along Cross Street to Trinity Street and walk down the path to the right of Poulton Hall, a former Methodist Chapel. This is Borough Well Lane and leads down to the Town Well (1) that provided the public with water from Roman times until 1923.

Continue along the lane to Bridge Street and turn right. This was a busy commercial area in Victorian times with many pubs and shops in evidence. Of particular note is No. 34, the Music House (2), where French statesman and author Chateaubriand took refuge from the revolution in 1797. Cross the bridge to reach the former Falcon Inn (3) on the corner and turn right into Falcon Lane.

Pass through a kissing gate into Falcon Meadow and follow the grassy path to re-cross the River Waveney over a weir to Bungay Staithe (4) (staithe – landing place or wharf). Until 1934, when navigation ceased, this area brought considerable wealth to Bungay for it was here that the local oak trees were used in the construction of wherries, the East Anglian sailing barges.

Walk on past Mill House (5), ceasing production in 1960, and right along Staithe Road past the flint faced almshouses (6) built in 1848 by Eliza Dreyer for poor widows. Turn right along Trinity Street to Holy Trinity Church (7) with its round tower, the oldest complete structure in the town. Continue on towards the town centre and turn left through the churchyard of St. Mary's (8) and the ruins of the Benedictine Priory founded by Gundreda, widow of Hugh Bigod, in 1160.

The church dates from the 12th century and was severely damaged in the Great Fire. It is famous for the legend of the Black Dog which, during a storm in 1577, was reported by Abraham Fleming to have terrified the congregation. Turn right out of the gates on St. Mary's Street to return to the Butter Cross.

For the western route walk into Market Place where a weekly market has been held since 1382, the King's Head and Three Tuns (9) are old coaching inns. The roundabout marks the site of the old Corn Cross, removed in 1809 and the town pump, removed in 1933. Turn left into Broad Street, noting the Fisher Theatre (10) on the right, opened in 1828 and later used as a corn exchange and now a centre for the performing arts. Further along on the right is Threshers (11), a building that survived the Great Fire.

Continue on to the Green Dragon (12), a pub that brews its own beer. Return back up the street past the now closed local cinema to the Waveney District Council Office and Town

Museum (13). Turn right through Cork Bricks, under the arch displaying the Black Dog, and right along Earsham Street, a street with a wide range of commercial premises and antique shops. At St. Mary's House Residential Home look across the street at the terrace of 17th century cottages (14) before continuing on down to Cock Bridge. Scott House (15), also called Bridge House, by the bridge was the home of John Barber Scott, 1792–1862, diarist and philanthropist.

Return back up the street as far as the Castles Inn (16) and turn right through the yard to the staggered metal barrier at the rear and the footpath to the castle (17). The twin towers were built in 1294 by Roger Bigod on the site of a former Norman castle built in 1165, information boards provide further details of the history and layout of the castle.

Follow the path out to Castle Orchard and right to Priory Lane to reach the main entrance to Castle Hills (18). These were earth works constructed by the Saxons to defend the town against the Danes and today provide fine views over the valley. Follow Priory Lane to St. Mary's Street and turn right to reach the junction of Upper and Lower Olland Streets. The motor accessory shop (19) at the junction is one of the few buildings to survive the fire of 1688, the name Olland is derived from 'off lands' i.e. off the main town thoroughfares.

Walk along Upper Olland Street past Nurseys (20) an old family shop specialising in sheepskin products that has celebrated its bicentenary and on to the Emmanual Church (21). This classic Congregational Chapel dates from 1818, the nearby tombstone of John Childs, the printer who broke the bible monopoly and enabled bibles to be sold cheaply, records his death in 1853.

Return back up the street and turn right through Turnstile Lane and left along Lower Olland and St. Mary's Street to Dinky's Garden (22), named after a pair of local fund-raisers who had a stall in the yard of the 16th century Angel Inn (23). Continue along St. Mary's Street to St. Edmunds RC Church (24), built in 1894 on the site of a small chapel opened in 1823. On the front of the building is a fine sculptural relief depicting the martyrdom of St. Edmund.

Continue on towards the town centre past the Fleece and the Swanson's Inns (25), two more of the town's old pubs, to reach the bakery opposite the Butter Cross. On the wall is a plaque marking the outbreak of the Great Fire of Bungay of 1688 and the end of the town trails.

Fact File

Location: Bungay is 40 miles north of Ipswich and 12 miles south east of Norwich
Start: The Buttercross Ordnance Survey map reference TM 336898
Length: 2¹/₂ miles
Conditions: Road and roadside footway, meadow – no stiles

How to get there:–
Public Transport: For details telephone Suffolk County Council's Public Transport Information TraveLine – 08459 583358
By Road: From Ipswich on A12 and A144 or from Norwich on B1332
Car Parking: Priory Lane, Lower Olland Street and others
Refreshments: A wide range of pubs, shops and restaurants are available in the town
Public Toilets: Priory Lane and Cross Street
Map: Ordnance Survey Explorer sheet 231 Southwold and Bungay
Reference: Bungay Town Trail by the Bungay Tourism Committee
Information: Waveney District Council Office, Museum and Information Point, Broad Street

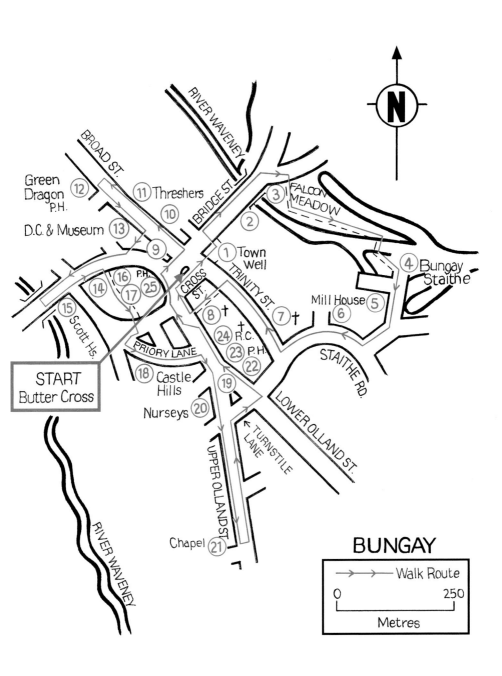

Green Dragon P.H.

D.C. & Museum

BROAD ST.

RIVER WAVENEY

BRIDGE ST.

FALCON MEADOW

(12)

(11) Threshers

(10)

(13)

(9)

(3)

(2)

(1) Town Well

(4) Bungay Staithe

CROSS ST.

TRINITY ST.

(14)

(16) P.H.

(17)

(25)

(15) Scott. HS.

(8) †

(24) R.C.

(23) P.H.

(22)

(7) †

Mill House

(5)

(6)

PRIORY LANE

STAITHE RD.

START Butter Cross

(18) Castle Hills

Nurseys (20)

(19)

LOWER OLLAND ST.

TURNSTILE LANE

UPPER OLLAND ST.

Chapel (21)

RIVER WAVENEY

BUNGAY

→—→— Walk Route

0   250

Metres

St. Edmund's Abbey

Abbeygate Street

4. Bury St. Edmunds

Bury St. Edmunds was once home to one of the most powerful monasteries in medieval Europe and has witnessed a great deal of turmoil over the centuries. The busy market town is now the cathedral town of Suffolk, situated at the centre of the west of the county, with its history and the giant abbey ruins now attracting visitors from all over the world. The abbey was built on the site of the shrine to the martyred Saxon King Edmund who rose to fame in the Middle Ages when St. Edmund became the patron saint of England.

The street plan is an example of early town planning, laid out in a rectangular grid pattern by Abbot Baldwin in the 11th century and is easily followed. The walk starts at Angel Hill by the Tourist Information Centre, opposite the Abbey Gate. There is much to explore in Bury St. Edmunds and this trail can only give you a taste of what can be found.

From the 15th to the 18th centuries Angel Hill was the scene of the Bury Fair, but disbanded by 1871 due to rowdyism and squalor. In the north corner, next to the Georgian style council offices, is a National Trust property (1), now the mayor's parlour. Walk through the Abbey Gateway (2), erected in 1347 after the former gate was destroyed in 1327, it has become the symbol of Bury St. Edmunds. The Abbey Gardens (3) beyond are splendidly kept, the flower beds and grass areas stretching down to the River Lark, once used as a navigation to the sea. Based on botanic gardens laid out by Nathaniel Hodson, they regularly win National awards for their bedding displays and are free to enter.

After exploring the gardens return to Angel Hill, on the opposite side stands the late 18th century Angel Hotel (4), featured in Dickens' Pickwick Papers and now regularly used as a backdrop to film and TV scenes. Walk left to the Athenaeum (5), at the end of Angel Hill, these 18th century Assembly Rooms provided the setting for two readings by Dickens and were opened in 1714 as a meeting house. Continue through Athenaeum Lane to the right and enter Chequer Square at the rear, dominated by the Norman Tower (6) and nearby Cathedral (7) across the road.

The tower was built in the 12th century, it is now the bell tower for the Cathedral Church of St. James, Suffolk's only Cathedral. Built in the 15th century, the Cathedral was restored by the Victorian architect Sir George Gilbert Scott. To mark the Millennium further work is being undertaken to provide the structure with a fine new tower in the centre of the building. Walk between the Cathedral and the Norman Tower to view the ruined arches of St. Edmund's Abbey (8) at the rear, now filled in to make unusual houses. On the lawn in front is a modern statue of St. Edmund by Elizabeth Frink and to the right at the meeting of pathways is an early 20th century memorial to Suffolk's martyrs of Queen Mary I's reign.

Return now to Chequer Square and turn left to reach St. Mary's Church (9), built in the 15th century to replace a previous church on this site, it contains the tomb of Mary Tudor, the sister of Henry VIII. Cross to Tuns Lane, leading into Bridewell Lane and turn right to Churchgate Street. Turn left along Churchgate Street with a variety of architectural styles from the 14th to 20th centuries, including the Unitarian Chapel (10). Standing behind wrought iron railings the building has been dated as 1712, and is regarded as one of the best remaining examples of unaltered chapel in the country. The lead rainwater hoppers are dated 1711, even though the building was not completed until 1712. Inside it houses galleries, box pews and a unique double-decker pulpit.

Turn left into Whiting Street to reach the United Reform Church (11). Turn right into College Lane, also known as Hogg Lane, at the side of a large 15th century half-timbered house to reach Guildhall Street. Turn right past the end of Churchgate Street to the 14th century Guildhall (12), once rented to the Guilds of the area by the Abbot and finally transferred to the town at the dissolution of the Abbey by Elizabeth I in July 1569. Although the 15th century roof remains, much of the brick facade dates from 1806.

Continue on to the end of Guildhall Street to arrive at the Corn Exchange (13), built by Ellis and Woodward in 1861 with massive cast iron roof trusses made by Ransomes and Sims of Ipswich. Pass around to the right into The Traverse where you will find the Nutshell (14), recorded in the Guinness Book of Records as the smallest public house in the country. Further along on the right is The Cupola House (15), a fine 17th century house with balcony built by Thomas Macro and capped by a cupola. Behind the current Corn Exchange is the former Corn Exchange (16), built in 1836 and enlarged in 1848, it was once the home of the Corporation Fire Engine.

At the end of The Traverse stands the Market Cross (17), on the site of the old Market Cross. Designed as a theatre in 1774 by Robert Adam, it has been used as the Town Hall and since 1970 as an art gallery. Turn right in Cornhill, formerly called Beasts Market and across to Moyses Hall (18), a Norman dwelling house dating from 1180. This building has been used as a house, a hostelry, jail, house of correction and the parcels office of the Great Eastern Railway. It is now the Borough Museum and houses a collection of exhibits of local interest. The clock tower was designed by Sir George Gilbert Scott.

Return to Abbeygate Street along the Butter Market (19), a wide street with an interesting variety of shops that are part of the town's main shopping area. Turn left along Abbeygate Street (20), the main pedestrianised thoroughfare through the town and containing a wide variety of well preserved old shops and business buildings, to return to the start of the walk at Angel Hill.

Fact File

Location: Bury St. Edmunds is 27 miles north west of Ipswich
Start: Angel Hill, Ordnance Survey map reference TL855642
Length: 1¹/₂ miles
Conditions: Town paths and road, no steps

How to get there:–
Public Transport: For details telephone Suffolk County Council's Public Transport
    Information TraveLine – 08459 583358 or Anglia Rail – 08700 402020
By Road: A14 from Ipswich and Cambridge, follow Tourist Information signs
Car Parking: Angel Hill Pay and Display car park, free on Sunday and Bank Holidays, or use
    other car parks within the town
Refreshments: The town supports a wide range of facilities such pubs, restaurants and shops
Public Toilets: Abbey Gardens and others
Map: Ordnance Survey Explorer sheet 211 Bury St. Edmunds and Stowmarket
Reference: Based on A Walk Around Historic Bury St. Edmunds, a booklet by the
    Bury St. Edmunds Society available widely in Bury St. Edmunds
Information: Bury St. Edmunds Tourist Information Centre – open daily except on Sundays
    November to Easter

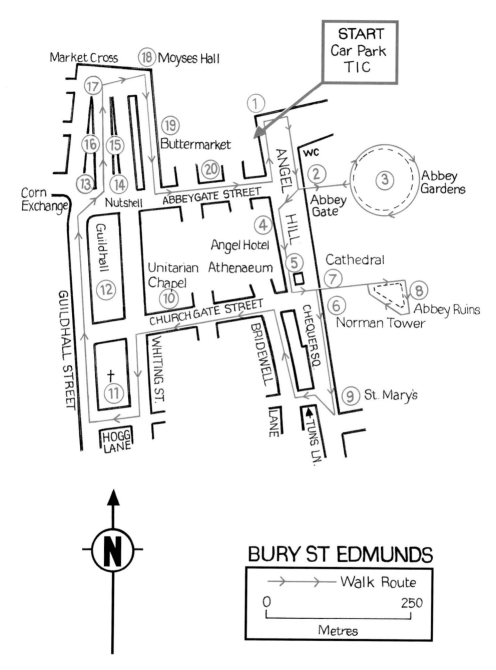

START
Car Park
TIC

Market Cross ⑱ Moyses Hall
⑰
⑲ Buttermarket
⑯ ⑮
⑳
⑬ ⑭
Corn
Exchange
Nutshell ABBEYGATE STREET
① ANGEL
wc
② Abbey Gate
③ Abbey Gardens
Guildhall ④ Angel Hotel
ANGEL HILL
Unitarian Chapel Athenaeum
⑤ Cathedral
⑫ ⑩ ⑦
CHURCH GATE STREET
⑥ Norman Tower
⑧ Abbey Ruins
GUILDHALL STREET
WHITING ST.
BRIDEWELL
CHEQUER SQ.
† ⑪
⑨ St. Mary's
HOGG LANE
LANE
TUNS LN.

N

BURY ST EDMUNDS

Walk Route

0   250
Metres

Church of St. Peter and St. Paul

Broad Street

5. Eye

The name Eye derives from an old Saxon word for island and it can be seen that the castle, church and old medieval town are raised above the surrounding flat land that were once water and marsh. In the 1850s Eye was a thriving town with an iron works, flax making, lace industry and a number of breweries.

From the Cross Street car park turn left past the Queens Head pub to the Town Hall (1), designed by the London architect E. B. Lamb in 1857. The bell in the clock tower is thought to be the original Sanctus Bell from the church. On the left is the Red House (2), a fine town house with 19th century red brick facade, both this and the White House next door once belonged to the Tacon family, local brewers.

Walk along Lambseth Street and across the tributary of the River Dove to the long crinkle crankle wall – (3) on the left, behind which stands Chandos Lodge built in 1811 and the home of Sir Fredrick Ashton, one time director of the Royal Ballet. Return towards the town and pause to look at the Bedingfield Almshouses (4), dating from 1850, the inscriptions read 'Believe right; Doe Well; Avoid Ill for Heaven, Amen; Povertie; Humilitie, Patience and Charitie'.

A few more steps and you will come to Linden House (5) behind a row of lime trees. This 17th century house was given a brick front in 1710 and was the home of Margaret Thompson, one of Emily Pankhurst's suffragettes. Walk along Broad Street to the junction with Church Street. The chemists shop on the corner (6) is a timber framed building of several dates, the oldest part dating from 1460 and other parts from 17th, 18th and 19th century.

Turn left along Church Street, a street of varied Victorian houses, many built around medieval structures, to the new arch (7) over the entrance to the Buckshorn Lane car park. Turn left opposite the arch down the narrow lane to Vine Church (8), a Baptist chapel built of white brick and with grapevine detail at either side of the central window. Continue along the curve of Church Street to No. 28 (9) on the right, a 13th century open hall house, rebuilt in the 18th century and one of the first in Eye to have sash windows, instead of the usual leaded lights. No. 53 (10) on the left with brick Dutch gable ends, reminding us of the trade links with the Low Countries.

The Primary School (11) dates from 1911 and carries the town's old coat of arms on the front. A grammar school was established here in 1495 with lessons held in the Guild Hall until school rooms were built in 1875. Next door stands the Guild Hall – (12) dating from the 15th century. The building was much restored by the Victorians but the corner post still has its medieval carved figure of the Archangel Gabrial and two carved window heads intact.

The magnificent church of St. Peter and St. Paul (13) was mostly built in the 14th century, although there was a church here in the 13th century. Inside is an intricately carved wooden rood screen with richly painted kings, saints and bishops. The roof is partly painted and, like many other parts of the church, partly restored in 1869 giving an idea of what it would have been like in the Middle Ages.

Pass through the semi circular churchyard and out to Castle Street, turning right to Stayer House (14). This is another medieval hall house with 16th, 17th and 19th century additions, including the porch supported by Ionic columns and on the left side, a private banking hall. Continue on to Nos. 31 and 33 (15), one of the few remaining thatched houses in Eye, originally three houses in 1590 and thatched in straw.

Turn right up Castle Hill, to the left are modern houses (16) built on the site of the original inner bailey of the castle which in 1794 was the site of a new workhouse for 350 poor and homeless people. To the right is Castle Mound (17) where there are information boards; climb the steps to the castle (18), built after 1066 by William Mallet and having a long history of change. In 1173 it was attacked by Hugh Bigod, Earl of Norfolk, rebuilt and again attacked in 1265, starting its decline. It has been used as a prison, its materials stolen for local building and in the early 19th century had a windmill on the top. What is left today are the remains of a folly and a house built by Sir Edward Kerrison for his batman who had saved his life at Waterloo. There is a superb view of the surrounding countryside from the viewing platform on the top.

Return to Castle Street and turn right to Stanley House (19), a 16th century timber framed house, once a private school and the home of the painter Cavendish Morton until 1978. At the road junction turn right to No. 18 (20) on the left, the former Horse Shoes pub displaying a small ceramic plaque with the Lacons brewery sign. There were once two breweries, 14 pubs and 5 beer houses in the town, only the Queen's Head remains. Next door is Harwen House (21) a red brick property with limestone detail, once used by a charity to distribute to the poor at Christmas.

On the next corner stands the Midland Bank (22) with a facade of sandstone, turn left into Magdalen Street, named after a medieval leper hospital in the area. Turn right in the entrance to Grampian County Foods to the former white painted Eye Station building (23), all that is left of the terminus of the Eye branch line. The 3 mile branch from the main line junction at Mellis was opened in 1867 bringing passengers and goods through a halt at Yaxley to the town. Passenger services were withdrawn in 1931, apart from a few specials, and the station finally closed to freight in 1964.

Return to the town centre and turn left into Broad Street where a market (24) was established soon after 1066. The memorial is dedicated to Sir Edward Kerrison MP for Eye from 1853 to 1866 and was designed by James Colling in 1888. Across the road is the White Lion (25), a former 15th century coaching inn, through the archway is the Eye theatre housed in the former assembly room. Walk through the gap to the left of the Co-op store to The Cross to return to the start of the trail at the Cross Street car park.

Fact File

Location: Eye is 19 miles north of Ipswich and 22 miles south of Norwich
Start: The Cross Street car park Ordnance Survey map reference TM 144739
Length: 1¹/₂ miles
Conditions: Road and roadside footway, some steps

How to get there:—
Public Transport: For details telephone Suffolk County Council's Public Transport Information TraveLine – 08459 583358
Road Route: From Ipswich on A14 west, then north on A140
Car Parking: Cross Street and Buckshorn Lane
Refreshments: A variety of facilities, including one pub and shops
Public Toilets: Cross Street car park
Map: Ordnance Survey Explorer sheet 230 Diss and Harleston
Reference: Eye Town Trail leaflet by Mid Suffolk District Council, available from car park machines, Partridge & Lucas Estate Agents and the Volunteer Centre
Information: Local information boards and the Stowmarket T.I.C., tel. 01449 676800

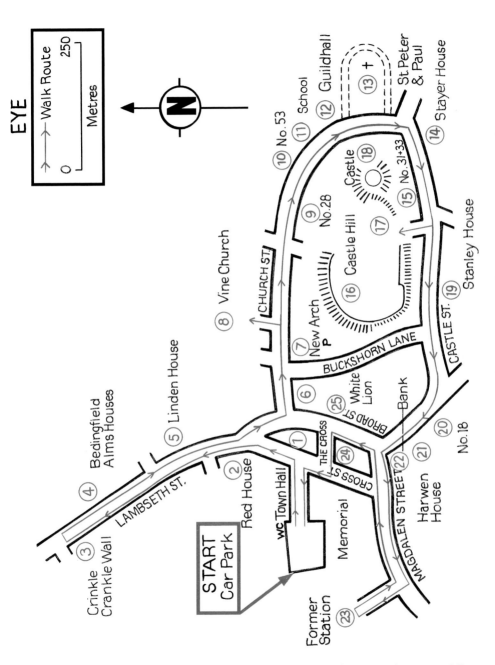

Great Eastern Square

Constable Cottage

6. Felixstowe

Although the Romans are connected with Felixstowe the main period of growth was in the late 19th and early 20th centuries when three particular aspects of the town developed. The oldest part of the town is centred around the old parish church of St. Peter and St. Paul. The second area was developed by the Cobbold family along the sea front and around Cobbold's Point. Finally the more industrialised part of the town developed to the south and was developed by Colonel Tomline, the Victorian entrepreneur.

This town trail is based on a booklet entitled The Cotman Walk, A Town Trail by the Felixstowe Society, for an in depth account it is recommend that a copy of this very interesting publication is obtained. The walk around the town enables you to see almost all the buildings designed by Thomas Cotman (1847–1925), the nephew of the John Cotman (1782–1842) the Norwich water colourist. Thomas Cotman lived in the Little Bungalow in Quilter Road and is buried in the churchyard of the old parish church in Old Felixstowe.

The trail starts from the forecourt of Great Eastern Square shopping precinct and the Town Railway Station (1). The railway first came to Felixstowe when a passenger service to the original Felixstowe Pier (now part of the docks) was opened by the Felixstowe Railway and Pier Company in May 1877. However, the company was purchased by Great Eastern Railway and, as the town developed, they opened Felixstowe Town station in 1898. The old Pier Station closed to passengers in 1951 and the intermediate Beach Station closed in 1959. British Rail has since also sold off the fine red brick Victorian Town Station building, now refurbished as a shopping precinct by the Ipswich Co-operative Society. The operational station is just a section of the remaining canopied open platform.

Look left across the road to the Orwell Hotel (2) on the corner, once the property of Douglas Tollemache the brewer and founder of Tolly beer. Turn right down Hamilton Road and past St. Andrews Road to turn left into Gainsborough Road, the northern boundary of the town's conservation area stretching to Hamilton Gardens on the cliff top. As you walk along the road note the typical Victorian houses (3), turn right in Constable Road and walk the length of the road to see Cotman's Little Bungalow (4), No. 3 in Quilter Road. Return back along Constable Road to St. Andrews Road and bear right to Brook Lane.

Turn right, on the other side of the road stands Constable Cottage (5), a farmhouse remodelled by Cotman, opposite are the four Brook Cottages designed by Cotman in 1891. Turn right along Bath Road, lined with several Victorian seaside houses with a variety of balconies (6). Pause at the Stable Block (7), designed by Cotman and built for the Bath Hotel.

At the end of the road, turn left down Bath Hill, the building on the left at the entrance to the Bartlet Hospital is all that remains of the Bath Hotel (8), burned down by Suffragettes on 22 May 1914. Two of the Suffragettes responsible for the fire and other sites in the area, Hilda Birkett and Florence Tunks were put on trial at the Town Hall on the sea front. They were later found guilty at the Suffolk Assizes and sentenced to 2 years and 9 months respectively. This was the last major outrage committed by the Suffragettes, women over the age of 30 were finally given the vote on 6 February 1918.

Continue along Undercliff Road East and look up to the left at the Bartlet Hospital (9), built on the foundations of a Martello tower. Further along is the Fludyer Arms, named after Sir Samuel Fludyer, a resident of Felix Cottage, and to the left the stables (10), now a tearoom and part of the pub premises but designed by Cotman, probably in 1904.

As the road bends up away from the sea front the building to the right was Cobbold's Point (11), Felix Cobbold's summer home, re-modelled by Cotman around 1885. The house was renamed Cranmer House in 1946 and is now private residences with no public access. Across the road and a little higher up is a red brick tower, ornate brick wall and gateway, all that remains of the Cobbold's stables (12), designed by Cotman in 1900 but unfortunately burned down in 1973.

Retrace your steps to the sea front and back to Beach Road East, turn up the hill to Atholl House (13), opposite the turning to High Beach. This house was designed by Cotman and built in 1893, note particularly the splayed base to the stairway tower, an effect Cotman had been seeking in other buildings. Walk to the end of High Beach, noting the crescent of houses with Georgian doorways, particularly the last house on the left (14) with balconies and a steamboat like appearance.

Return to the sea front again and turn right to walk back up Bath Hill. Walk past the front of the splendid Harvest House (15), formerly the Felix Hotel and designed by Cotman for Douglas Tollemache in 1903. Turn left along Cambridge Road to Hamilton Gardens (16) where there is a good view of the gardens at the rear of Harvest House and of the pier, first opened in 1905. Continue past Cliff House (17) with its dominating position on the cliff top and on, past a variety of interesting architecture to reach the top of Bent Hill. In 1933 a Mr. P. Harris of Ipswich managed the rare feat of riding his cycle backwards up the hill.

Turn right along Hamilton Road, continuing up through the town, taking note of the variety of architecture. Of particular note are Barclays Bank (18) with a wealth of detailed decoration and sympathetically restored and, on the next corner, Lloyds TSB Bank (19). This was designed by Cotman in 1870 and built in 1890, it stands on the site of the very first shop in Felixstowe.

To complete the walk continue on along Hamilton Road, passing the Town Triangle (20), usually with a colourful display of summer flowers and on down the wide street to return to the start of the walk at Great Eastern Square.

Fact File

Location: Felixstowe is 11 miles south east of Ipswich
Start: Felixstowe's Great Eastern Square, Ordnance Survey map reference TM 304351
Length: 2^1/$_2$ miles
Conditions: Roadside footway and road throughout, very easy walking

How to get there:‒
Public Transport: For details telephone Suffolk County Council's Public Transport Information TraveLine ‒ 0645 583358 or Anglia Railways ‒ 08700 402020
Road Route: From Ipswich on A14, follow the signs for the station
Car Parking: Easy parking in several car parks around the town
Refreshments: A wide range of facilities for all tastes
Public Toilets: Undercliff Road East, The Triangle Hamilton Road and many others
Map: Ordnance Survey Explorer 197 Ipswich, Felixstowe & Harwich
Reference: The Cotman Walk, A Town Trail and Walking Around Felixstowe by the Felixstowe Society, available locally cost £1.50
Information: Felixstowe Tourist Information Centre ‒ open all year daily

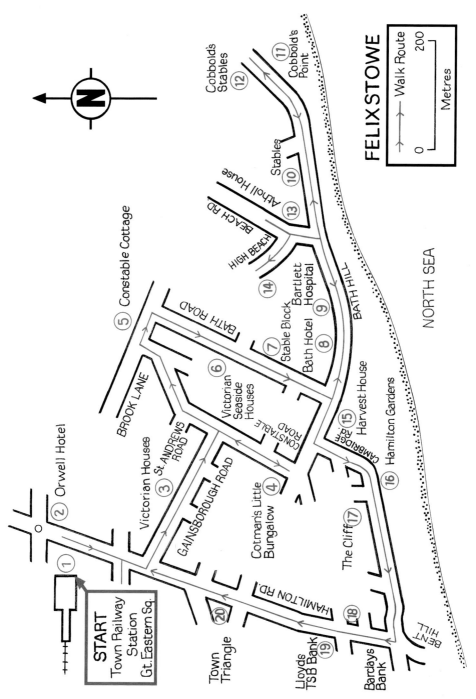

FELIXSTOWE

→ Walk Route

0   200
Metres

NORTH SEA

Cobbold's Stables

⑪ Cobbold's Point
⑫

Stables
⑩

Atholl House
⑬

BEACH RD.

HIGH BEACH

⑭

Stable Block
⑦ Bartlett Hospital
⑨
Bath Hotel
⑧

BATH HILL

Constable Cottage
⑤

BATH ROAD

BROOK LANE

Victorian Seaside Houses
⑥

CONSTABLE ROAD

Harvest House
⑮

Hamilton Gardens
⑯

Orwell Hotel
②

Victorian Houses
③ St. ANDREWS ROAD

GAINSBOROUGH ROAD

Cotman's Little Bungalow
④

CAMBRIDGE Rd.

The Cliff ⑰

①

START
Town Railway Station
Gt. Eastern Sq.

Town Triangle
⑳

HAMILTON RD.

Lloyds TSB Bank ⑲

⑱

Barclays Bank

BENT HILL

Reproduced from Ordnance Survey mapping on behalf of The Controller of Her Majesty's Stationery Office © Crown Copyright. Licence Number AL100037826.

Hitcham's Almshouses

Framlingham Castle

7. Framlingham

Framlingham's history has centred around the castle since 1100 AD and benefited from the prosperity of the powerful families of the Earls and Dukes of Norfolk, receiving its grant of a market in 1286. It is recorded that there had been a 7th century Anglian settlement surrounded by a wooden stockade on a site to the left of the drive leading to the castle and there is evidence that there was a church in this area, possibly the one mentioned in Domesday Book. The town's population has generally remained stable at around 2,000 to 3,000 over the past 130 years, in spite of recent new housing that has taken place, leaving the town a popular tourist attraction.

The trail starts from the Elms car park, walk to the main entrance on New Road, opposite the Hitcham's Almshouses (1) built in 1654 to house 12 poor people. The Masonic Hall at the end was formerly a school and was added in 1789. Turn left to Well Close Square and on along the street to Albert Place (2) at the junction with Fore Street. Look back for a fine view of the United Reform Church, the oldest part of which was once a flourmill and became a Methodist Chapel in 1885. Note the pump by the river, once the town's principle water supply, it has two spouts that enabled the tall water carts to be filled to supply outlying houses, whilst the lower spout was used by the townspeople to fill buckets and cans etc.

Continue along Station Road past the Mills Almshouses (3), completed in 1709, six years after the death of Thomas Mills, a devout Baptist and wheelwright. After crossing Brook Lane you will find Tomb House (4), the tomb in the garden was erected over the grave of Thomas Mills who died in 1703 and, as he was a dissenter, was not buried in the churchyard.

Cross the street and, before returning on the other side, look up the road to see the Station Hotel (5) next door to the site of the former station. Framlingham was connected to the East Suffolk line by a 5^1/$_2$ mile branch line from Wickham Market junction with its terminus at Framlingham. The line opened on 1st June 1859 with regular passenger traffic finishing in 1952, although special school trains continued to use the line together with freight traffic until the line finally closed in April 1965. The station buildings of Framlingham and intermediate stations at Parham and Marlesford have survived and are in use as offices and private houses etc.

Return along Station Street past the Railway Inn (6), another reminder that the town was linked to the railway network, and walk on to Fore Street. Turn right over the river and, at the end of the railings of Durley House, turn left into Queen's Head Alley (7). The black and white half timbered building at the top of the path was once the Blue Boar and later, from about 1800, the Queen's Head, probably referring to Queen Mary who came to Framlingham to take refuge. Follow the path up through the arch, thought to be the original toll entrance into Framlingham, into the triangular Market Hill (8). Records indicate that a market has existed here since 1270 and is still operating at least once a week.

Turn left, noting the buildings on the left, and the archway that now provides an entrance to the Solar store that would once have allowed passage for carriages. At the Town Sign (9), depicting local scenes, cross to the raised pavement area in front of the shops opposite and turn right up the steps. The main building housing these shops was once the Guildhall (10) and the raised pavement area marks the boundary of the former Mansion House that once stood on the site.

The Crown Inn (11) at the top of Market Hill was a coaching inn on the route from Ipswich to Norwich and until the 1950s there was an opening at the front to allow the coaches through from Fore Street. The 18th century front replaces the original Tudor Inn, constructed of wattle and daub and on view inside. Turn left into Church Street and then right into Double Street (12), originally called Bow Street. This is thought to mark the inner moat of a former motte and bailey castle, believed to have been located about where the Castle Inn stands today. Follow the curving road round to the junction with Castle Street, noting the red Victorian pillarbox (13) on the left. Turn right along Castle Street to reach Jeaffreson's Well (14) at the junction with Badingham Road and Saxmundham Road. The well was sunk in 1896 in memory of local doctor William Jeaffreson F.R.C.S. and his wife, it had a tank fitted in the roof to feed the local houses, although now disused.

Return back along Castle Street on the opposite side of the road past The Readery (15), the home of The Reader who gave bible readings to the inhabitants of the Almshouses. Continue on to the Ducking Pond (16) opposite the Castle Inn, in the 17th century a large number of witch trials took place in Framlingham. Turn right up the drive to the castle to reach the gate in the castle wall (17). The curtained walled castle dates from the 12th century probably replacing the earlier wooden castle nearby in the previous century. The monument is now administered by English Heritage and includes the Lanman Museum containing artifacts from the town's history.

Return down the drive past the Castle Inn and along Church Street to reach the main entrance to the Churchyard. Turn right through the wrought iron gateway to reach the church door. The church (18) is well worth a visit to view the tombs of the Howards, a 15th century wall painting and the splendid Tamar Organ built in 1674. Follow the path down a few steps and along Church Lane out to Market Hill.

Turn right along Bridge Street, noting the library (19) housed in the former Court House of 1872 and in use as Judge's Courts until 1924 and as a Magistrate's Court until 1978, and the Unitarian Meeting House of 1717 next door. Cross the River Ore and turn right on the path to the right of the modern Elms housing complex to return to the Elms car park at the rear. The Mere (20) at the rear of the car park is thought to be a natural feature, is owned by Framlingham College, managed by Suffolk Wildlife Trust and fed by the River Ore.

Fact File

Location: Framlingham is 19 miles north of Ipswich and 7 miles west of Saxmundham
Start: The Elms car park off New Road, Ordnance Survey map reference TM 283635
Length: 1¹/₂ miles
Conditions: Town footways, very easy walking, a few steps

How to get there:-

Public Transport: Check for details with Suffolk County Council's Public Transport Information TraveLine 08459 583358
By Road: From Ipswich north on A12 to Wickham Market, then B1116 to Framlingham
Parking: Free parking at The Elms car park off New Road
Refreshments: There are several public houses, shops, restaurants and other facilities in the town
Public Toilets: Crown and Anchor Lane
Map: Ordnance Survey Explorer sheet 212 Woodbridge and Saxmundham
Reference: Framlingham Town Trail leaflet by Framlingham Town Council
Information: Volunteer Centre and Library on Bridge Street or the Castle's Lanman Museum

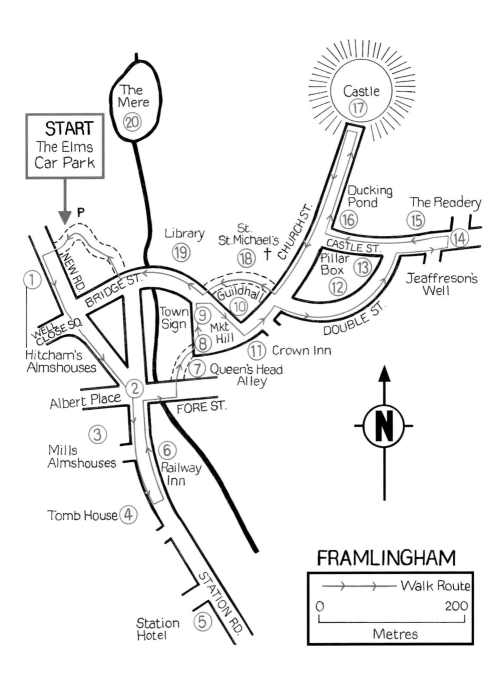

START
The Elms
Car Park

The Mere
20

Castle
17

Ducking Pond
16

The Readery
15

Library
19

St. St.Michael's
18

CHURCH ST.

CASTLE ST.

Pillar Box
13

Jeaffreson's Well

14

NEW RD.

BRIDGE ST.

Guildhall
10

12

DOUBLE ST.

1

WELL CLOSE SQ.

Town Sign

9

Mkt Hill
8

11 Crown Inn

Hitcham's Almshouses

2

7 Queen's Head Alley

Albert Place

FORE ST.

N

3

Mills Almshouses

6

Railway Inn

Tomb House 4

FRAMLINGHAM

→——→—— Walk Route

0   200

Metres

STATION RD.

Station Hotel

5

The Coffee Tavern

Guildhall

8. Hadleigh

Over 600 years ago Hadleigh was one of the region's most important wool and market towns and by the 16th century was only surpassed in richness by Bury St. Edmunds and Ipswich. The town has an important architectural history originating in Saxon times. The 9th century Danish King Guthrum is reputed to be buried in the town which has been placed with 51 other towns of national concern by the Council for British Archaeology as 'so precious that ultimate responsibility for them should be a national concern'.

The trail starts from the Library and Tourist Information Point at the junction of Duke Street and High Street. Turn left along the High Street, lined with merchant's houses dating from periods from the 15th century. The former White Lion pub **(1)** was once the most important inn in the area, the medieval structure is covered with 18th century bricks and rendered, whilst within is a small courtyard.

The George Inn **(2)** was one of the town's main coaching inns and retains some of the features that allowed access for the coaches. In the 18th century a gang of smugglers used the inn to receive contraband and in the last century the mail coach brought the mail from London in about 10 hours.

George Street and Church Street once formed the main crossroads in the town and is marked by the old obelisk milestone recording the distances to nearby towns. A few more yards along the High Street is the Coffee Tavern **(3)** with Venetian windows and a richly decorated 17th century front.

Continue along the High Street noting the Victoria Wine shop **(4)** with its pargetted decoration and, beyond Angel Street, the brickwork of Tye House, No. 99 displaying a royal coat of arms, the medieval door of Sun Court and at the very end of the street, The Old Forge **(5)**.

Turn left along Bridge Street, on the left is the Old School **(6)**, a former Victorian Church of England school and on the grass on the other side of the road, a preserved section of the old cast iron bridge that once spanned the River Brett. Turn left into the car park before the bridge and follow the path to the footbridge over the river to Corks Lane.

The red brick offices of Babergh District Council **(7)** are an adaptation of medieval and Georgian houses and 19th century maltings and designed by Ove Arrup Partnership who were the consulting engineers for the Sydney Opera House. Turn left along Corks Lane, parallel to the river, to the start of the Riverside Walk **(8)** on the left. This is a pleasant surfaced ½ mile footpath beside the River Brett with views through the trees of the church and Deanery Tower and leading on to the Toppesfield Bridge **(9)**.

The medieval bridge was a toll bridge and important route for the wool trade. It was widened in the 16th century and is registered as an Ancient Monument. Cross the road and follow the white railings along Tinkers Lane at the edge of the river. Opposite Mill House turn left and cross the footbridge at the site of Hadleigh Mill **(10)**, Tinkers Lane crossed the river via a ford a few yards downstream, follow the path and you will rejoin the old lane up to Benton Street.

Turn right, noting the variety of quaint old buildings and, at the corner of Raven Way, the Flying Chariot **(11)**, an old pub decorated with the original plaster and ornate carved timbers. Continue along Benton Street and turn left up Cranworth Road and, at the end, walk up the steps to the top of the railway embankment. Turn left towards the town passing the cast iron National Cycle Network milestone, along the way there are superb views over the valley, river and Holbecks Park.

The 7^1/$_2$ mile railway (12) ran from the junction with the main line at Bentley through stations at Capel and Raydon to the terminus at Hadleigh. Although the line was opened in 1847 it was originally planned to extend on to Bury St. Edmunds, but closed to passengers in 1932 and finally closed in 1965 under the Beeching cuts. To view the old station (13) and the surrounding buildings, turn right up Station Road and right into Station Yard.

Turn left down Station Road to the war memorial (14) and then right along the High Street. Turn left into Duke Street and then right at the first turning into Market Place (15). At the right bend there is a view of the 17th century Toppesfield Hall (16) on the left, now the headquarters of the East Anglian Tourist Board.

Turn left at the colonnaded Corn Exchange (17), built on the site of a bullring, and walk through to the open area of the churchyard. On the left is the three storeyed Guildhall (18), a series of timber framed buildings dating from the 14th century. The upper floors projected over the ground floor, known as jetties, and were a sign of wealth and status. The building has had many uses including a grammar school and is currently the offices of the Town Council, using the original 1619 council chamber.

To the west of the church is the Deanery Tower, built with ornamental battlements by Archdeacon Pykenham in 1495 while Rector of Hadleigh, as a gatehouse for a planned mansion. The circa 1240 St. Mary's Church (19) is one of the largest parish churches in East Anglia, has had additions in 1440 and a Victorian roof to the nave. The spire and 14th century Angelus Bell, one of the oldest in East Anglia, dominates the surrounding town and brings this town trail to a conclusion.

There are many other interesting buildings and places to visit in the town if you can spend more time to browse around. To return to the start, walk along Church Street to the High Street and then right to the start of the trail at the library.

Fact File

Location: Hadleigh is 9 miles west of Ipswich and 9 miles east of Sudbury
Start: Hadleigh Library, Ordnance Survey map reference TM 027423
Length: 3 miles
Conditions: Roadside footways and surfaced paths, some steps, sometimes muddy after rain
How to get there:–
Public Transport: Check for details with Suffolk County Council's Public Transport Information TraveLine – 08459 583358
Road Route: From Ipswich west on A1071
Car Parking: There is plenty of free parking in the town, the main car park entrances are off Magdalene Road
Refreshments: There is a wealth of pubs, shops, restaurants and other facilities in the town
Public Toilets: Magdalen Road
Map: Ordnance Survey Explorer sheet 196 Sudbury, Hadleigh and Dedham Vale
Reference: A Visitor's Guide to Hadleigh by the Harry Smith Trust, 50p from library
Information: Hadleigh Tourist Information Point at the library, local bookshops have books and leaflets about Hadleigh

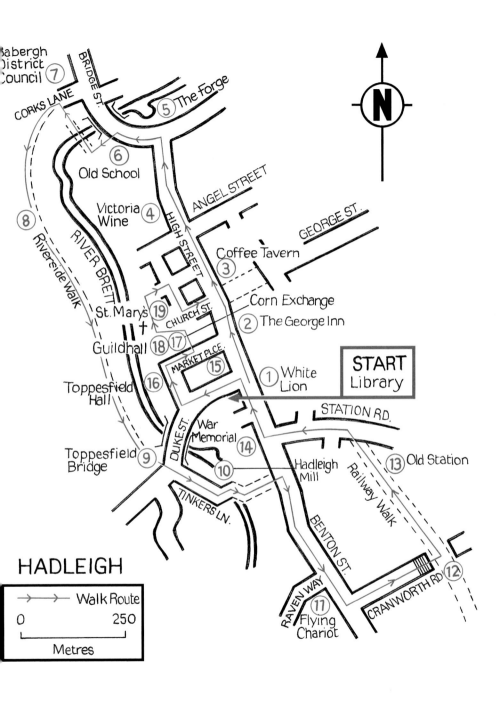

HADLEIGH

Walk Route

0 — 250

Metres

The Almshouse

Town Quay

9. Halesworth

The market town of Halesworth expanded rapidly in the 18th century when it was connected to Southwold by the canalised River Blyth. A century later further expansion took place when the East Suffolk Railway brought about a more rapid form of transport, connecting the town with Ipswich and London.

Start your walk from the Angel Hotel (1), an ancient coaching inn that has also been used as the town's court and council meeting place. Opposite is an ornate terracotta fronted building (2) originally designed as a bank. Turn left and follow the road around the corner to the Arboretum (3) and war memorial, developed on the site of a house that burnt down in 1899. Next door, along the Thoroughfare, are the Parish Rooms, used by the town council until 1977, and at the next junction, the former White Lion pub (4), previously also called The Boar and in use until 1966.

The walk has now reached London Road, known as Pound Street until 1880 and the original location of a pound where the Lord of Halesworth Manor kept stray animals. Numbers 1 and 2 (5) on the left were built in the 15th century and later became one house as the home of the Bedingfield family until 1705. From 1816 to 1889 the house was Harvey's Academy for Boys.

Turn right up Steeple End to the former Almshouse (6), funded by money left by William Carey who stipulated that it house 12 poor single men and women. Across the road is St. Mary's church (7), of Saxon origin and recorded in the Domesday Book, with Ulf the parish priest. Turn right by the church and follow the path through to the Market Place.

At the top of the market to the left stands the former Three Tuns pub (8), a 16th century building that was once a post house and is currently the Halesworth and District Social Club. On the other side of the market stands an Italiante style building (9) that was a department store until the 1960s and now houses a number of shops. The building to the right of these shops is the former Mansion House (10), birthplace of Sir Benjamin d'Urban, Governor of the Cape of Good Hope who gave his name to the city of Durban. To the left of the shops is an archway where old flax and hempworks buildings (11) can be seen, later used for stabling by the department store.

Turn left along Chediston Street (12), where there were once many pubs and small breweries, the area was known as Cherry Bow. After a short distance turn right into the narrow Rectory Lane, noting the charming crinkle crankle wall (13) on the right. After crossing the river the Old Rectory can be seen behind the wall on the left, part 16th century with 18th and 19th century additions. One former occupant of the rectory from 1822 to 1831 was Rector Richard Whately, a critic of slavery who became Archbishop of Dublin in 1831. The actor Kevin Whately is a descendant.

On reaching Rectory Road turn right to Bridge Street then left past the new library, crossing the road by the former Hawk pub (14) to the shops opposite. The open land behind these buildings was the site of the former Suffolk Carriage Works that in 1868 employed 100 people and later built motor cars to special order.

Cross Saxon Way to Hooker House (15) on the other side. Originally Brewery House, it was the home of Sir William Hooker, renowned botanist and the first director of Kew Gardens. It is also the birthplace of Sir Joseph Dalton Hooker who was the second director of Kew Gardens and a close friend of Charles Darwin.

Cross Quay Street to the United Reform Church (16) and turn left around the corner to Norwich Road, walking up the hill to turn right along New Cut. The large brick building on the left is the former Prince of Wales Brewery (17), soon to be developed as New Cut Arts. Turn left up Station Road (18), a street with an interesting mix of houses, Magnolia House on the left was the home of Sir William Aitken MP.

At the top of the road stands Halesworth Station (19), built in 1859 and now housing the Halesworth Museum. In 1888 the station was provided with a moveable platform, designed to allow traffic along the road, and restored in 1999. This was also once the junction with the Southwold branch line that opened for business in 1879 until it finally closed in 1929. It was planned to extend the Mid Suffolk Light Railway from Haughley on the Ipswich to Norwich main line to Halesworth on the East Suffolk line. However, construction only ever reached Cratfield near Laxfield and the Middy, as it was known, closed for business in 1952.

Return down Station Road to Quay Street and turn left for about 50 metres. Turn right into the wide access approach to Ridgeons, walking through the steel arch over the path between the fences to a bridge over the river. This is the site of the original Town Quay (20), once a bustling area that supported five public houses and many storage areas for the coal, iron, corn, bricks, timber and other goods carried on the river. The first boat arrived from Southwold in 1761, laden with coal and shortening the journey time considerably. However, the river gradually became silted up and the new railway took on most of the transport business in the area with the result that the last boat arrived in 1882.

Follow the path over the second bridge into the Town Park (21) and straight on to the underpass under Saxon Way by the side of the river, eventually emerging in the Thoroughfare. Before 1300 much of this area was flood plain and details of the early history can be found in the Halesworth Museum. In the Thoroughfare there are examples of 15th, 16th, 18th and 19th century buildings. No. 6 (22) with the carved beam over the door is believed to be 14th century and the home of Dame Margery, the widow of Lord of the Manor Richard de Argentein, the beam carries part of the de Argentein coat of arms.

Turn left up the Thoroughfare to a block of four shops on the left that are housed in a building that was once the Guildhall (23). Built in 1474 it housed the Guild of St. John the Baptist and Guild of St. Loye and St. Anthony. A few more steps up the Thoroughfare and you are back at the start of the walk at the Angel Hotel.

Fact File

Location: Halesworth is 25 miles north east of Ipswich, 12 miles south of Beccles
Start: Halesworth Angel Hotel
Length: 1 mile
Conditions: Town footways and road, no steps or stiles

How to get there:—

Public Transport: Check for details with Suffolk County Council's Public Transport Information TraveLine – 08459 583358 or Anglia Railways – 08700 402020
By Road: From Ipswich north on A12 and A144 to Halesworth
Car Parking: Town centre pay and display car parks off Saxon Way and Angel Link
Refreshments: Wide range of facilities for all tastes in the town
Public Toilets: Market Place, Norwich Road and Town Park
Map: Ordnance Survey Explorer sheet 231 Southwold and Bungay
Reference: Halesworth Town Trail leaflet produced by the Halesworth Town Trail Project with the help of the people of Halesworth and the Halesworth and District Museum
Information: Halesworth Museum and Waveney District Council office – London Road

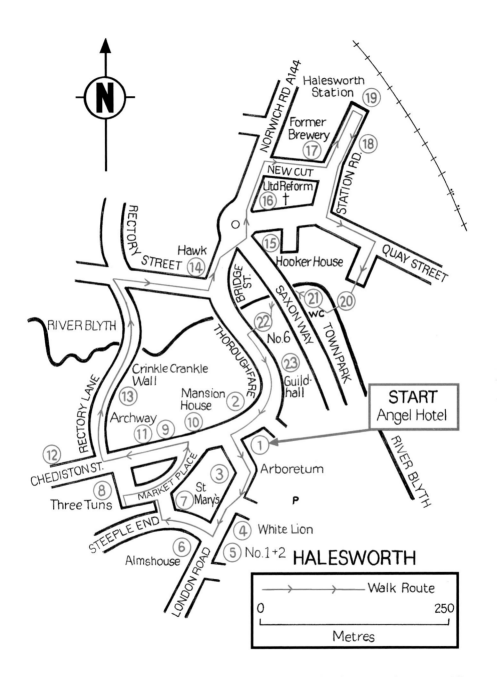

N

Halesworth Station ⑲
NORWICH RD A144
Former Brewery ⑰
⑱
STATION RD.
NEW CUT
UtdReform ⑯ †
QUAY STREET
Hawk ⑭
RECTORY STREET
⑮
Hooker House
O
BRIDGE ST.
SAXON WAY
RIVER BLYTH
⑳
⑳
WC
THOROUGHFARE
⑳
No.6
Crinkle Crankle Wall
RECTORY LANE
⑬
Mansion House ②
⑳
Guild-hall
TOWN PARK

START
Angel Hotel

Archway
⑪ ⑨ ⑩
⑫
CHEDISTON ST.
①
Arboretum
RIVER BLYTH

MARKET PLACE
③
St Mary's
P
⑧
Three Tuns
⑦
STEEPLE END
④ White Lion
⑥
⑤ No.1+2 **HALESWORTH**
Almshouse
LONDON ROAD

Walk Route
0   250
Metres

Reproduced from Ordnance Survey mapping on behalf of The Controller of Her Majesty's Stationery Office © Crown Copyright. Licence Number AL100037826.

Town Hall Arts Centre

Old Independent Church

Former Cangle School

10. Haverhill

Haverhill (meaning hill where oats are grown) stands in the south west corner of Suffolk and is bounded by the counties of Essex and Cambridgeshire on its southern and western sides. After a fire swept through in 1667 little remains of the old medieval town, although between 1951 and the present day it has quadrupled in size, following its nomination as an 'expansion town' by the Greater London Council.

The town has the proud distinction of having been a market town for 950 years and, as you will find on this walk, has evolved as a centre of non-conformity. It was through the textile industry that the town became prosperous, particularly in the latter part of the 19th century. By the end of the 18th century, the cloth trade was in decline in East Anglia but was revived by the introduction of two new fabrics, silk and drabbet, a coarse, hardwearing material, used for working clothes. Whilst silk brought only modest wealth, Haverhill became famous for its drabbet smocks.

The great watershed in Haverhill's history was the building of a factory containing 32 power looms by D. Gurteen and Sons, a company that has been in the town since the 1780s. Between 1851 and 1901 the town almost doubled in size, producing a complete Victorian town with new houses, schools, churches and public buildings.

The town trail starts from the Town Hall, now a thriving Arts Centre and the last stop on our exploration. Walk up the High Street and Hamlet Street to the Old Independent Church (1) built in 1884 for one of the town's two oldest non-conformist congregations. Opposite stands Weavers (2), one of the few remaining medieval houses in the town.

Return back towards the town and turn left up Colne Valley Road to Vanners (3), a fine red brick silk weaving factory built in 1865, with managers houses attached at each end. Return to Hamlet Road and turn left, noting the original shop fronts on the right (4). Turn left at Duddery Hill, the original White Hart Inn (5) stood much closer to the corner but was pulled down because there was a danger to traffic. Turn right into Helions Walk and continue on at the end along the footpath to reach the Ex-Serviceman's Club.

Bear right down Quaker Lane (6), the house behind the wall on the right was once the Quaker Meeting House (7), was built in 1833, has several gravestones in the garden but has now been converted to private dwellings. On the other side of the lane is Gurteen's factory (8). Continue down to the High Street and note the first shop on the left, Chapman and Son (9) formerly the Market Hill Chapel. This was built in 1839 when a section of the Old Independent Church congregation broke away and then later also built the West End Congregational Church.

Continue left along the High Street and note the old Co-op building (10) on the right, now housing Argos and built in 1897 at a cost of £3,400. Carry on along Queen Street noting the old shop fronts (11) and on to the junction with Wratting Road and Withersfield Road. On the left is the Rose and Crown pub (12) that served the livestock market situated behind it. Across the road is the Old Cangle School (13) where virtually all the local children went from the time it was opened in 1877 at a cost of £5,313. It is now closed and is to be turned into a community centre and flats by St. Edmundsbury Borough Council. To the right and up the hill is Station Road, the station opened in 1865 to bring the Great Eastern Railway and greater prosperity to this part of the town.

Continue along the Withersfield Road to the Corn Exchange (14) built conveniently near the new market in 1889 and now housing the St. Felix Club. Carry on to the West End Congregational Church (15), the Sunday School was built first in 1890 followed by the church and manse to complete the trio of buildings. The original organ from the Original Independent Church is now housed here.

Just beyond the church complex turn left up the narrow path of Downs Place and note the terrace of three storied weavers cottages (16) on the right. Turn left at the top and walk along the edge of the old livestock market, now a car park at the rear of the Corn Exchange (17) and pub. At the end of the former market bear right on the path between fences, to the right of Lower Down Slade car park, to reach the red brick Downs Baptist Chapel (18). This is the oldest surviving Non-Conformist church in the town, was built in 1828 and paid for by local collections.

Continue along Upper Downs Slade to Camps Road and turn left down to the old market place (19). There is a Tourist Information Point in the library that is worth visiting for further information. On the right of the old market place stands the medieval market town church of St. Mary's (20) complete with tiny churchyard. The damage caused to the church during the great town fire of 1667 was finally put to rights when the burnt out shell was restored in 1864, leaving little remaining of the original medieval structure. Take the path to the right of the church to reach the High Street, noting the original red brick Corn Exchange on the corner.

Turn right along the High Street, passing the modern shop fronts, to reach the Town Hall Arts Centre (21). This was built in 1883 by Daniel Gurteen who also added the tower and spire to the Original Independent Church that we saw at the start of the walk. The building was refurbished in 1994 by St. Edmundsbury Borough Council and provides services to the community. Take a look inside at the modern stained glass window at the entrance by Catrin Jones and use the facilities and refreshments on offer to complete your walk. The main hall is on the upper floor and has been fitted with a unique terraced seating system that can be automatically folded back when the hall is required for dancing etc.

Fact File

Location: Haverhill is 32 miles west of Ipswich
Start: Town Hall Arts Centre, Ordnance Survey map reference TL 673453
Length: 1¹/₂ miles (short cuts available)
Conditions: Roadside footway and town paths, no stiles

How to get there:—
Public transport: For details telephone Suffolk County Council's Public Transport Information TraveLine − 08459 583358
By Road: From Ipswich west on A1071 and A134 to Sudbury, then A134, A1022 and A604 to Haverhill, from Cambridge on A1307 and A604
Car Parking: Pay and Display at South Town Centre (Town Hall) car park
Refreshments: Plenty of pubs, shops and takeaways etc. in the town.
Public Toilets: Town Hall and at other locations
Map: Ordnance Survey Explorer sheet 210 Newmarket and Haverhill
Reference: Information supplied by the Haverhill and District Local History Group
Information: Tourist Information Point at the library off Camps Road

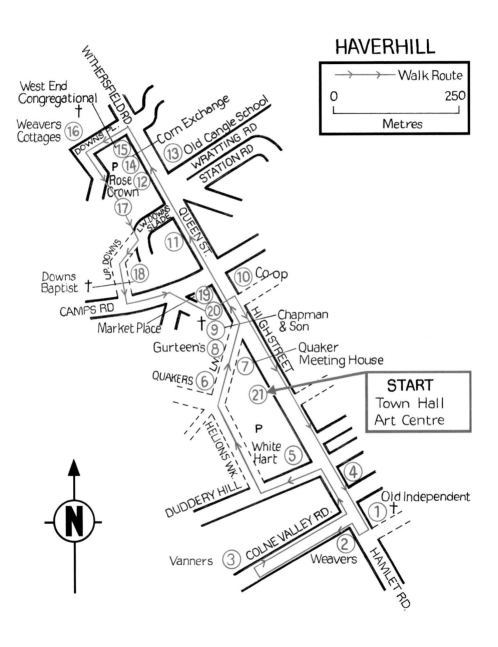

HAVERHILL

Walk Route

0   250

Metres

West End Congregational ✝

Weavers Cottages ⑯

WITHERSFIELD RD

DOWNS PL.

Corn Exchange

Old Candle School

⑬

WRATTING RD

STATION RD

⑮

P ⑭

Rose Crown ⑫

⑰

L.W. DOWNS SLADE

UP. DOWNS

QUEEN ST.

⑪

Downs Baptist ✝

⑱

CAMPS RD

⑩ Co-op

Market Place

⑲

⑳

Chapman & Son

⑨

HIGH STREET

Gurteen's ⑧

✝

Quaker Meeting House

QUAKERS ⑥

⑦

L.W.

START
Town Hall
Art Centre

㉑

P

White Hart ⑤

HELIONS WK.

DUDDERY HILL

④

Old Independent ✝ ①

COLNE VALLEY RD.

Vanners ③

Weavers ②

HAMLET RD.

N

Ipswich Museum

Malt Kiln pub and Isaac Lord warehouse

11. Ipswich

Suffolk's county town of Ipswich takes its name from the Old English Gippeswick and is clearly steeped in a long history, too detailed for one town trail. This trail is therefore a taster, based on the Historic Waterfront Trail and returns to the start via a number of other interesting buildings.

The trail starts at the Ipswich Museum (1) in High Street where you will find the first of a series of pavement plaques directing you down the hill to Crown Street. Turn left along Crown Street to the pedestrian crossing at Crown Pools but before crossing, note The Cricketers pub (2), built to reflect the style of Helmingham Hall, the home of the Tollemaches, and the former owners of the brewery.

Cross Crown Street and head down Lloyds Avenue to the arch (3) built in 1931. Under the arch are plates set in the pavement with distances to places in East Anglia. On the other side of the arch is the Cornhill (4) with two grand 19th century buildings, the Town Hall on the right and former Post Office on the left.

Turn left along Tavern Street passing the end of The Walk (5) and The Thoroughfare, built in the 1930s with mock Tudor alleyways. At Dial Lane glance left up Tower Street at St. Mary-le-Tower (6), a civic church as long ago as 1200 and rebuilt in the 19th century.

Turn right into Dial Lane and, just before reaching the Buttermarket, note the little coffee shop (7) on the left, once Scarborow's Optician, as can be seen by the spectacle like front windows and the pair of wrought iron frames incorporated into the gate. As you cross the Buttermarket take time to view the splendour and decoration of the 15th century Ancient House (8) before continuing down St. Stephen's Lane. Pass between the Tourist Information Centre in St. Stephen's Church (9) and the main entrance to The Buttermarket shopping centre, to Dogs Head Street.

Across the road is the bus station on the site of The Old Cattlemarket (10) from where it gets its name. Turn left along Dogs Head Street to the junction with Upper and Lower Brook Street and across the pedestrian crossing to Tacket Street. The road soon opens out with Christ Church Baptist church (11) on the left and then, on the corner of Foundation Street, the former Unicorn pub and brewery (12). Look up for a view of the splendid unicorn weather vane. Continue on through Orwell Place to Fore Street (13), on one corner is the ironmongers Martin and Newby, established in 1873 and an Alladin's cave for DIY enthusiasts. Across the road is the Eagle pub one of the few ancient pubs to survive.

Turn right down Fore Street, so called because it was the foremost or principal street of the area. At the junction with Lower Orwell Street note the old stone work remains of Blackfriars Monastery (14) in the shadow of the new red brick flats, and then a little further down the street, the distinctive Ipswich Oriel windows of the wine merchants, Heyman, Barwell & Jones.

Cross the busy Star Lane via the pedestrian crossing and continue along Fore Street, taking note of the blue plaque on No. 44 (15), in memory of the Dutch artist Cor Vissar. Next is the Fore Street swimming baths (17), built in 1894 with funding from Felix Cobbold. To the left there is a view of St. Clement's Church (16), the burial place of Sir Thomas Slade who designed the flagship Victory.

Turn left past the Lord Nelson pub (18) and cross the road via the pelican crossing. Turn right then left around the corner into Salt House Street. Turn left into Wherry Lane, past the John Russell Gallery, and out onto the waterfront of the Wet Dock which is the end of the marked

Waterfront Trail from the museum. However, if you don't want a long walk, turn right to the Old Customs House (24), and continue with the description at ★ below.

The terminus of the Waterfront Trail is actually at the old Tolly Cobbold Brewery (22), some distance to the left, past the Wet Dock Lock Gates. Turn left along Wherry Quay, passing the Malt Kiln pub (19), a former 17th/18th century malting and the Issac Lord (20) complex of merchant's house, weaving sheds and warehouses. Next comes Neptune Quay providing mooring for modern craft in the marina within the dock and Copralite Street (21), the site of the former Fisons Fertilizer works.

Continue down the side of the dock and look out over the 35 acres of this unique basin that, when it was opened in 1842, was the largest area of enclosed water of its kind in England. Soon you will see the lock gates at the end of the dock marking the exit to the River Orwell. Walk to the end of Eagle Wharf at the end of the quay and turn left along Ship Launch Road. Turn right along Cliff Road, bearing left just before the Cliff Quay dock gate, into the car park of Tolly Cobbold's old Victorian brewery (22). Return back along Cliff Road and then turn left into Patteson Street, at the site of the old gas works, to return to the waterfront.

★ Turn right and walk to Common Quay and the magnificent Old Custom House (23), built in 1842 and now the headquarters of the Ipswich Port Authority. Continue along Albion Wharf, under the extended canopies of the maltings and mills, to the end of the water of the wet dock. Turn right on Foundry Lane to College Street and then turn left, past the red brick of the Wolsey Gate (24) which served the school founded by Wolsey in 1528.

Cross the street to St. Peter's Church (25) and across Star Lane to reach St. Peter's Street. Look out for a view into St. Peter's Court (26) on the right. On next to St. Nicholas Street, noting the modern red brick Cardinal House (27) on the left, built on the site of the Hippodrome Theatre. Turn left into Cromwell Street, now a car park, and then right at the side of the black glass Willis Carroon Group building (28). To the right is the Unitarian Meeting House (29), built in 1699 at a cost of £257.

Turn left at the corner of the Willis Carroon building to cross Princes Street and on to Museum Street. Walk up Museum Street glancing left down Elm Street for a sight of the red brick Tudor church of St. Mary at the Elms (30) and then down Arcade Street at the arch. Opposite the Museum Street Methodist Church note the huge colonnaded facade of the former Ipswich Museum (31) building. Continue up the street, crossing Westgate Street and Crown Street to return to the start at the Museum (1) in High Street, opened in 1881.

Fact File

Location: Ipswich is 27 miles east of Bury St. Edmunds and 40 miles south of Lowestoft
Start: Ipswich Museum, Ordnance Survey map reference TM 161449
Length: 3 miles
Conditions: Roadside footways – very easy walking

How to get there:–
Public Transport: For details telephone Suffolk County Council's Public Transport Information Service – 08459 583358 and Anglia Railways 08700 402020
By Road: From A14 and A12 follow signs for town centre car parks
Refreshments: A wide variety of pubs and shops in the town
Public Toilets: Several in the town
Map: Ordnance Survey Explorer sheet 197 Ipswich, Felixstowe and Harwich
Reference: Various leaflets reproduced by kind permission of Ipswich Borough Council
Information: Ipswich Tourist Information Centre open Monday to Saturday

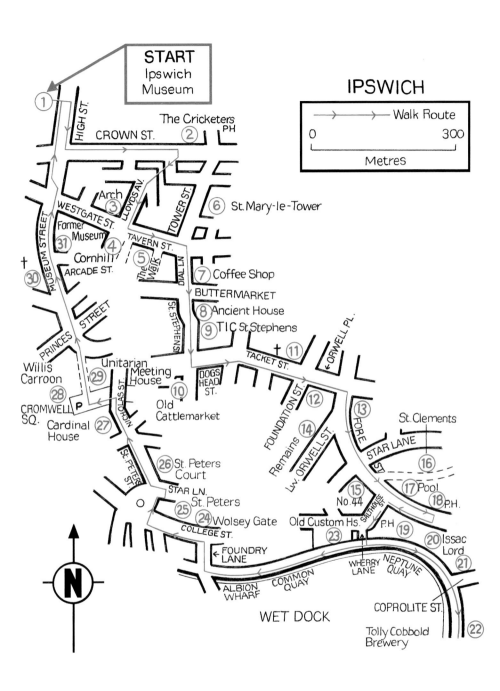

START
Ipswich
Museum

IPSWICH

Walk Route
0   300
Metres

① HIGH ST.
CROWN ST. ② The Cricketers PH
Arch ③
LLOYDS AV.
Former Museum ㉛
WESTGATE ST.
TOWER ST.
⑥ St.Mary-le-Tower
MUSEUM STREET
Cornhill ④ TAVERN ST.
ARCADE ST. ⑤ The Walk
† ㉚
DIAL LN.
⑦ Coffee Shop
BUTTERMARKET
⑧ Ancient House
⑨ TIC St Stephens
STREET
PRINCES
ST.STEPHENS
† ⑪
TACKET ST.
ORWELL PL.
Willis Carroon
Unitarian Meeting House ㉙
DOGS HEAD ST.
⑩
⑫
⑬
St.Clements
CROMWELL SQ. ㉘
NICOLAS ST.
Old Cattlemarket
FOUNDATION ST.
FORE
Cardinal House ㉗
P
⑭ Remains
Lw.ORWELL ST.
STAR LANE
⑯
ST.PETER
㉖ St.Peters Court
⑰ Pool
⑱ P.H.
O ㉕
STAR LN.
⑮ No.44
SALTHOUSE ST.
St.Peters
㉔ Wolsey Gate
Old Custom Hs.
P.H ⑲
⑳ Issac Lord
COLLEGE ST.
㉓
㉑
FOUNDRY LANE
WHERRY LANE
NEPTUNE QUAY
ALBION WHARF
COMMON QUAY
COPROLITE ST.
N
WET DOCK
Tolly Cobbold Brewery
㉒

Long Shop Museum

Haylings Pond

12. Leiston

The meaning of the first element of the name Leiston (Old English leah or leg + tun) is unclear and it is possible that it could mean 'Farmstead in the clearing' or alternatively 'Beacon-fire farmstead'. One mile to the north of the town stands the ruins of Leiston Abbey, founded by the Premonstratensian Order in 1182 at Minsmere, rebuilt in the 14th century and destroyed in 1536. However, the chapel has been restored and is still in use and the ruins, the most extensive monastic remains in Suffolk, are open to the public.

Leiston owes much of its later development to the Garrett Engineering Works, established in 1778 and one of the earliest agricultural machinery manufacturers in the country, continuing operations until it ceased in 1980. The Long Shop was one of the earliest examples of flowline production and has been restored by the Longshop Trust. The original works now form the Long Shop Museum and houses exhibits of Garrett's agricultural and wartime products, including a Garrett anti aircraft gun.

The trail starts from the Sizewell Road car park, turn right and walk to the crossroads at High Street and Cross Street with the Black Horse pub (1) on the corner. Turn right into High Street passing the ornate front of the United Reform Church (2) on the right and a variety of small businesses lining the street, eventually turning left into Post Office Square (3).

The former works house (High Green) faces the Main Street on the left and dates from 1820 to 1830. It consisted of the Drawing Office and Head Office and has now been converted into five houses in an award winning scheme aimed at converting surplus industrial buildings. The Long Shop Museum (4) is also on the left and well worth a visit to view much of the town's history. The old Post Office opposite is now the library and the Town Council Offices. Walk on past the Engineers' Arms (formerly much used by Garrett workers) and turn right by the White Horse Hotel on the B1122 to reach the railway crossing and former station (5).

The branch line from Saxmundham opened in 1859 and extended on to Aldeburgh in 1860, enabling excursions from London to Aldeburgh to run until 1939. The line finally closed for passengers in 1966, although freight to Aldeburgh had ended in 1959. Leiston Station is now a private house although goods traffic to the Sizewell Halt, just outside Leiston, continues to serve the Sizewell power stations.

Return to the crossroads at the White Horse Hotel and turn right to the Quaker Meeting House (6). The first meeting house was built in 1735 but the present structure dates from 1860 with improvements undertaken in 1989. At the rear is a small Burial Ground with simple gravestones displaying all-numerical dates; the Quakers objected to the names of the days and months dedicated to pagan gods.

Walk up Waterloo Avenue, past the Middle School, formerly the Secondary Modern and Grammar Schools. Turn left into Church Road to reach Leiston Church (7), named after St. Margaret of Antioch and one of three churches mentioned in Domesday Book. The church was designed by E. B. Lamb and rebuilt in 1854. There is a 13th century font and five bells in the tower dating from 1640 to 1674. In the churchyard there are three iron head-stones made locally by Garretts whilst inside there are plaques to Richard Garrett, who died in 1866, and his family.

Behind the Church is Leiston Hall (8), with Dutch gables, which has now been converted into flats. At the end of Church Road follow the path on the left by the Church Hall. The Cupola (9), a large two-storey house in the trees on the right, was formerly owned by the Vannecks, the Lords Huntingfield and lords of the manor, although the cupola itself has gone.

By the second metal barrier take the right fork in the path between the trees and bushes and then walking alongside a high chain link fence and a field edge. Turn left into the housing estate past the front of the first three houses, turning right on Beech Walk and left on Ashfield Drive to reach Haylings Road. Turn left for about 30 metres to a lane to the right of Fridays Orchards, marked with a footpath sign, and head for the old Water Tower (10), now converted to a private house. Bear right through the gateway half way down the lane into the public open space of Haylings Pond, crossing diagonally right around the pond to an exit in the far corner. Turn right along the path to join Goldings Lane.

Turn left along the lane to the junction with the Aldeburgh Road. To the right are the Ogilvie Homes (11), sheltered housing built in 1887 and recently enlarged. Turn left along Aldeburgh Road and then right into Red House Lane. Red House farmhouse (12) was built in 1720, but has been much altered and extended.

Walk to the Leiston Leisure Centre (13) at the end and turn left on the road at the side of house number 51, just before the main entrance. Where the road bends left continue straight on along the path between fences and gardens to emerge in Quakers Way (14) by a pair of old cottages. This is the site of the old Quaker burial ground, purchased in 1670, there is reputed to be a stone in the garden of one of the cottages to mark the burial ground.

Turn left as far as the junction with South Close and then right past a telephone box to Seaward Avenue. Turn left and then right on Sylvester Road to the Fire Station (15) and Community Day Centre. Turn left along Sizewell Road past the Crown Inn to return to the start of the walk at the Sizewell Road Car park.

Fact File

Location: Leiston is 27 miles north east of Ipswich
Start: Sizewell Road Car Park – Ordnance Survey map reference TM 447625
Length: 3 miles (plenty of short cuts)
Conditions: Roadside footway, field edge paths, grass and tracks, muddy when wet, no stiles

How to get there:-
Public Transport: Check details with Suffolk County Council's Public Transport Information TraveLine – telephone 08459 583358
Road Route: From Ipswich on A12 north to Saxmundham and then B1119 to Leiston town centre
Car parking: Pay and Display at Sizewell Road car park or free at Post Office Square (limited to 1 hour) and other on street parking
Refreshments: A wide variety of pubs and shops in the town
Public Toilets: Sizewell Road and off Post Office Square on Dinsdale Road
Map: Ordnance Survey Explorer sheet 212 Woodbridge and Saxmundham
Reference: Leiston Suffolk, 2 Circular Walks – leaflet produced by Leiston Leisure Learners Local History Group
Information: Longshop Museum open April to November, Leiston Library and local shops

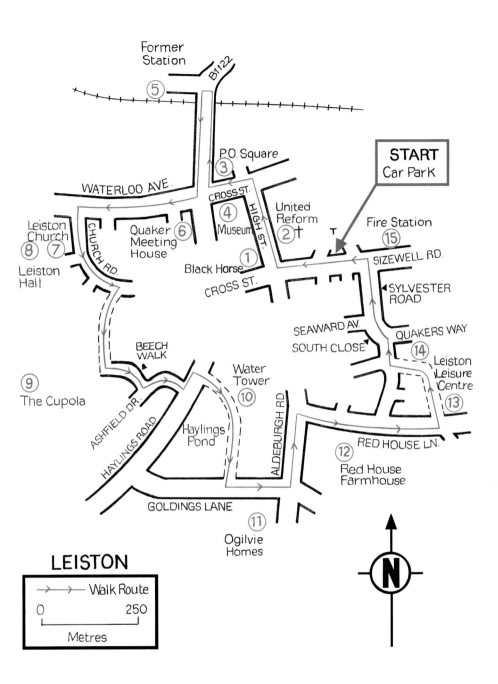

Former Station

B1122

⑤

START
Car Park

P.O. Square

③

WATERLOO AVE.

CROSS ST.

④

HIGH ST.

United Reform

②†

T

Fire Station

⑮

SIZEWELL RD.

Leiston Church

⑧ ⑦

Leiston Hall

CHURCH RD.

Quaker Meeting House

⑥

Museum

Black Horse

①

CROSS ST.

SYLVESTER ROAD

SEAWARD AV.

SOUTH CLOSE

QUAKERS WAY

⑭

Leiston Leisure Centre

⑬

BEECH WALK

Water Tower

⑩

ASHFIELD DR.

HAYLINGS ROAD

Haylings Pond

ALDEBURGH RD.

RED HOUSE LN.

⑨
The Cupola

⑫
Red House Farmhouse

GOLDINGS LANE

⑪

Ogilvie Homes

LEISTON

→—→ Walk Route

0   250

Metres

N

Old Blue Anchor Stores pub

Town Hall

13. Lowestoft

Lowestoft was established by the Danes, is Britain's most easterly town and is often known as the 'Town of the Rising Sun'. It has a sea-faring tradition based on fishing, its port and more recently the oil and gas industry, as well as being a holiday resort. The town is divided by the river and Lake Lothing that serve as an inner harbour, providing access to Oulton Broad and acting as a gateway to the inland waterways. The north side of the town contains most of the area's history and therefore this town trail explores that part of the town. However, the south side was developed by Sir Samuel Morton Peto in the 19th century as a holiday resort to rival Brighton and a leaflet describing the Peto Trail is available from the Tourist Information Centre in the East Point Pavilion.

The East Point Pavilion, also on the south side of the river, provides the start point for this trail. Walk north across the Lowestoft Bridge (1), the third bridge to be built at this point. The first was opened in 1830 when a cut was made from Lake Lothing to the sea, the second was opened in 1897 and called Victoria Bridge and the present structure was opened in 1972. Continue on to Station Square with the railway station (2) on the left, probably designed by John Thomas, erected in 1854 and resembling the original Norwich Thorpe station. On the right, on the corner of Waveney Road, stands the former Tuttles department store (3) with its ornate front.

Walk through the centre of the town along London Road North, now partly pedestrianised, to The Prairie (4), a narrow arcade on the left next to WH Smiths. This is so called because it is thought to have once been part of a private estate where deer roamed and is now part of the Britten Centre. At the junction with Gordon Road stands St. Margaret's Villa (5), built in the Italian style for the Rev. Charles Herbert, who was Rector of Lowestoft from 1860 to 1870. It later became the residence of Colonel Seppings JP, the first provisional Mayor of the town.

After passing the United Reform Church (6) built in 1852 we come to the Wheatsheaf pub (7) on the corner of Herring Fishery Score. The pub was once known as the Herring Fishery and was owned by the Old Company of Beachmen. This section of the town is built on the cliffs and access to the shore was through the many Scores or alleyways that lead down to the beach area. A leaflet describing the Lowestoft Score Trail is also available from the Tourist Information Centre.

Triangle Plain Market (8) was once the main shopping centre and marks the start of the High Street. The Old Blue Anchor Stores pub (9) stands on the corner of Dukes Head Street, formerly Blue Anchor Lane, and has the longest pub name in Lowestoft. On the right is Martin's Score (10) where an information board is displayed describing the Armada Post, put down to mark the defeat of the Spanish Armada 100 years after the event.

The Town Hall (11) dates from 1860 and is built on the site of the old Chapel of Ease, a curfew bell tolls out every night at 8 o'clock on a bell made from brasses taken from the parish church in 1644. The Royal Falcon (12) is looking a little less royal these days but was formerly North Flint House, said to have been built about 1551. It was once the home of Sir Thomas Allin, the Lowestoft Admiral, who on retirement bought Somerleyton House.

Walk on to reach the lighthouse known as High Light (13), given this name to distinguish it from the Low Light, the light that was on the beach until 1925. The lighthouse was opened in 1874 and became fully automatic in 1975. Coal was used to power the lights until 1788, then oil was used until 1938 when electricity was installed.

Cross Cart Score and enter Belle Vue Park (14), walking past the thatched lodge to the War Memorial (15). The park was the site of a battery of cannon, later becoming a communal drying ground until opening as a park 1874 when it was laid out as an arboretum. The war memorial was erected after World War II and stands on the site of a former bandstand, the three cannons probably represent the three batteries that once protected the town.

Turn left at the war memorial and then right across the Ravine Bridge (16), erected in 1887 to Commemorate Queen Victoria's Golden Jubilee. Turn right along North Parade to the corner and right down a set of steps to the Ravine at the junction with Cart Score. To the left is Denes Oval (17), the home of Lowestoft Cricket Club and once the town's allotments. Enter the Sparrow's Nest Park, where there is the opportunity for refreshments, and walk down past the Armada Beacon to the exit on Whapload Road. Turn right to the Lowestoft and East Suffolk Maritime Museum (18), housed in the bowling green cottage, formerly a house provided by the church for a churchwarden.

Continuing south, on the other side of the road are The Denes (19), an area marked with unique posts and rails used for hanging nets, ropes and fishing gear to dry. On the right are the old net stores and fish houses, now used for a variety of commercial purposes. Walk past the modern Birds Eye Walls frozen food factory (20), the modern way to deal with the products of the sea, and turn left along Wild's Street. At the junction of Newcombe Road you will find JT Cole (21), the last fish smoke house in the beach area.

Return to Whapload Road and turn left to Christ Church (22), built in 1869 for the beachmen and fishermen as a monument to the Rev. Francis Cunningham MA, a former vicar of Lowestoft. Continue on to Hamilton Road and turn left to view the Hamilton Dock (23), the last dock to be built and opened by Lord Claude Hamilton in 1903. Return to the roundabout and turn left along Battery Green Road, the site of the South Battery (24) where, in 1782, about 300 men manned a fort with 13 pieces of cannon.

Walk on past the Bethel fisherman's church (25) built in 1899 to Waveney Road with a good view of the Trawl Basin (26) through the railings. The Trawl basin was opened in 1865, to the north of it lies the Waveney Dock (27), opened in 1883 by Lord Waveney. Follow the roadside footway back over the Lowestoft Bridge to return to the start of the trail at the East Point Pavilion.

Fact File

Location: Lowestoft is 41 miles north east of Ipswich and 12 miles south of Yarmouth
Start: The East Point Pavilion Ordnance Survey map reference TM 547952
Length: 4 miles
Conditions: Road and roadside footway, some steps

How to get there:–
Public Transport: For details telephone Suffolk County Council's Public Transport Information TraveLine – 08459 583358 or Anglia Railways – 08700 402020
By Road: From Ipswich or Yarmouth via A12
Car Parking: Small car park at start, otherwise town centre car parks
Refreshments: A wide range of pubs, shops and restaurants are available in the town
Public Toilets: Triangle Plain, Sparrow's Nest, Battery Green Road
Map: Ordnance Survey Outdoor Leisure sheet 40 – The Broads
Reference: Trail details provided by Lowestoft Tourist Information Centre
Information: Lowestoft Tourist Information Centre – open daily all year

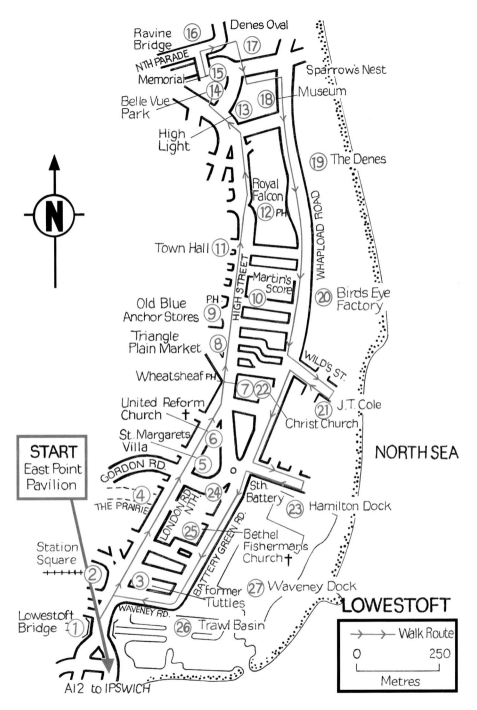

Ravine Bridge ⑯
NTH PARADE
Denes Oval
⑰
Sparrow's Nest
Memorial
⑮
⑭
Belle Vue Park
⑱ Museum
⑬
High Light

Royal Falcon ⑫ PH

⑲ The Denes

WHAPLOAD ROAD

Town Hall ⑪

HIGH STREET

Martin's Score
⑩

⑳ Birds Eye Factory

Old Blue Anchor Stores
PH
⑨

Triangle Plain Market
⑧

Wheatsheaf PH

WILD'S ST.

⑦ ㉒

United Reform Church †

㉑ J.T. Cole
Christ Church

St. Margarets Villa
⑥

NORTH SEA

⑤

GORDON RD.

START
East Point Pavilion

④
THE PRAIRIE

LONDON RD. NTH

㉔

Sth. Battery

㉓ Hamilton Dock

㉕

Bethel Fisherman's Church †

Station Square

BATTERY GREEN RD.

②

③

former Tuttles
㉗ Waveney Dock

LOWESTOFT

Lowestoft Bridge ①

WAVENEY RD.

㉖ Trawl Basin

A12 to IPSWICH

→ → Walk Route

0   250
Metres

Reproduced from Ordnance Survey mapping on behalf of The Controller of Her Majesty's Stationery Office
© Crown Copyright. Licence Number AL100037826.

63

Christ Church

Hawks Mill

14. Needham Market

Needham Market is situated between Ipswich and Bury St. Edmunds taking its name from Anglo Saxon 'Nied' meaning needy and ham meaning hamlet. The town trail starts and finishes at Needham Lake Picnic Site and is well signed from all directions. The Lake was created in the early 1970s when sand and gravel was extracted to build the A14 trunk road. Around the town you will find a number of blue plaques erected by the Needham Market Society to provided additional information.

From the Lake's Visitor Centre walk under the railway bridge and turn right towards the town. Pass Uvedale Hall (1), now a residential nursing home where the grandson of the noted botanist the Rev. Robert Uvedale lived. He is reputed to have introduced the Cedar Trees of Lebanon into England, several can still be seen around Needham Market, a result of seeds distributed by him.

At the Ipswich Road view the Old Grammar School (2), which was occupied by Lloyds Bank and a firm of solicitors. This timber-framed building dates back to the mid 17th century and was originally a school given to the town by Sir Francis Theobold. At the end of Station Yard is the railway station (3), built between 1846 and 1849 and designed by Frederick Barnes of Ipswich, the architect responsible for other notable local buildings in this Elizabethan and Jacobean style.

Between 1663–65 Needham Market was isolated due to the plague. Chains were placed across the roads at either end of the town to deter people from entering or leaving. The residential area to the south of the town (towards Ipswich) is called Chainhouse (4), deriving its name from the chains. The modern housing between Nos. 35–51 High Street (5) was built after a German bomb was dropped on the High Street in 1942.

On the right hand side of the High Street is Christchurch (6), rebuilt in 1837 as a congregational chapel in the Greek revival style. Joseph Priestley, who discovered oxygen, was appointed minister of the previous chapel in 1755. On the left-hand side of the High Street is the Old Town Hall (7), built in 1866 and designed by Frederick Barnes. Over the entrance is a stone tablet incised with date, patron, architect and builder.

The Causeway (8) marks the path once used to carry the dead to the cemetery at Barking, about 1 mile away. On the corner stands the almshouses, inside are two medieval carvings of figures, probably surviving from earlier buildings on the site. Behind the present Post Office (9) is a building that dates back to 1704 and was formerly the Quakers' Meeting House and graveyard, Needham Market was an important centre for the Society of Friends.

The former Bulls Head Inn (10) opposite the Post Office has a finely carved angel corner post dating back to the 15th century. The Limes Hotel (11) built around 1500 is a high quality timber framed building that in 1771 was encased at the front in red brick. It is thought that in the Middle Ages the inn was used by Pilgrims as a calling house on their way to Bury St. Edmunds. Tudor House (12) is typical of many 15th century timbered houses which lie behind altered facades in the High Street.

Crossing over the road, you can now more fully appreciate the Church of St. John the Baptist (13). The church was mainly rebuilt over the period 1486–1495, the fine double hammer-beam roof of the nave is one of the most outstanding of its type in England. Further up the High Street is Barclays Bank (14), built in the early 15th century, it was in this house that Samuel Alexander established his bank in 1744, one of the earliest private banks.

Turn right into Hawksmill Street. On the right hand side is the heavily timbered Ancient

House (15) built in the late 14th century. A tablet in the garden wall facing Hawksmill Street commemorates the Suffolk Show that was held in Needham Market in 1893.

Walk along the raised footway and down the steps leading under the railway bridge to Hawksmill (16), built in 1884. There has been a mill on this site since the Domesday Book was compiled, the brick building to the right replaced a wooden mill. Continue along the road to the entrance to Alder Carr Farm and turn right along the Tarmac pathway until you reach the footbridge over the River Gipping.

The river (17) was a navigable waterway as far back as the 12th and 13th century, when Caen stone was brought up the river to Rattlesden and then taken overland to build Bury St. Edmunds Abbey. The Ipswich and Stowmarket Navigation came into existence when an Act of Parliament was passed in 1790 to construct the navigation. The waterway opened in 1793, with 15 locks lifting the barges 90 feet over the course of 17 miles. The cargo ranged from slate, coal, timber and manure to chemicals and gun cotton. In 1846 the railway company leased the navigation for 42 years and increased tolls to encourage traffic to transfer to rail. The waterway was neglected and, when handed back to the canal company, in such a state that barges were unable to get to Stowmarket. The canal company went into liquidation and navigation was ended by Act of Parliament in 1932.

Cross the river via the footbridge to the roadway on the other side and turn left to reach a gate into Station Field. Keep to the left edge, past Kings Meadow Nature Reserve (18) on the town side of the river where there are a number of seats within the reserve from where you can observe a wealth of wildlife. From the reserve continue straight on across the grass to eventually meet the Tarmac path that circuits the lake. Turn left to reach the footbridge giving access over the river to the main car park.

Across the bridge and to the right is Bosmere Mill and Lock (19), built in the late 18th century, it has a large iron breast-shot water wheel which was formerly inside the wheelhouse. The lock next to the Mill has been restored by the Inland Waterways Association. The brick walls have been replaced, the copingstones realigned and in the future, it is hoped to reinstate the wooden lock gates so that a narrowboat can navigate the canal up to Hawks Mill.

Continue around the lakeside path to return to the start of the walk at the Visitor Centre.

Fact File

Location: Needham Market is 8 miles north west of Ipswich and 4 miles south east of Stowmarket

Start: Needham Lake Visitor Centre, Ordnance Survey map reference TM094546

Length: 1¹/₂ miles

Conditions: Roadside footway and riverside path, very easy − 1 stile (can be avoided)

How to get there:−

Public Transport: For details telephone Suffolk County Council's Public Transport Information TraveLine − 08459 583358 or Anglia Railways − 08700 402020

By Road: From Ipswich via A14 west to Beacon Hill (A140 junction), then follow signs

Car parking: Free at lake and in the town

Refreshments: A wide variety of pubs and shops in the town

Public Toilets: Needham Lake

Map: Ordnance Survey Explorer sheet 211 Bury St. Edmunds and Stowmarket

Reference: Needham Market Town Trail by Mid Suffolk District Council

Information: Needham Lake Warden's Office and Information Board, Mid Suffolk District Council, High Street and T.I.C. Wilkes Way, Stowmarket tel. 01449 676800

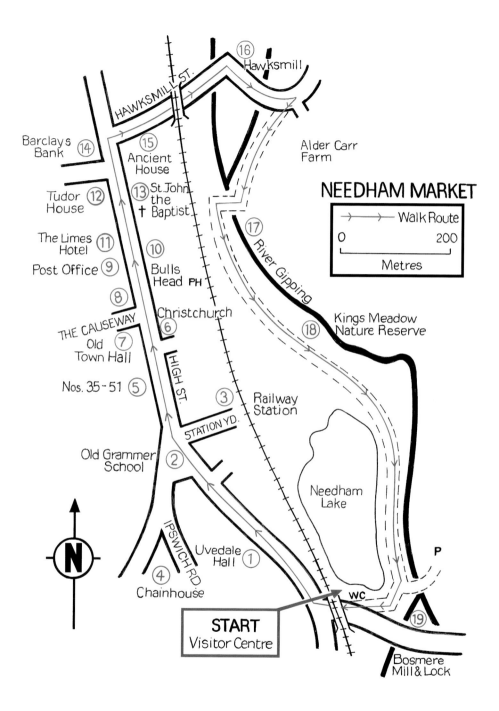

NEEDHAM MARKET

Walk Route

0   200

Metres

Hawksmill

16

Barclays Bank 14

Alder Carr Farm

Ancient House 15

St John the Baptist 13

Tudor House 12

The Limes Hotel 11

Post Office 9

Bulls Head PH 10

8

THE CAUSEWAY

Christchurch 6

Old Town Hall 7

Nos. 35-51 5

HIGH ST.

17

River Gipping

Kings Meadow Nature Reserve

18

Railway Station 3

STATION YD.

Old Grammer School 2

Needham Lake

IPSWICH RD.

Uvedale Hall 1

P

4

Chainhouse

WC

START
Visitor Centre

19

Bosmere Mill & Lock

N

Jubilee Clock Tower

Fred Archer's grave

Warren Hill Gallops

15. Newmarket

Geographically, Newmarket holds an unusual position. As the most westerly of Suffolk's towns it is nevertheless surrounded by Cambridgeshire parishes whilst still situated within the Suffolk county boundary. From the 17th century the town has become a metropolis of racing, home to the headquarters of the Jockey Club and boasting two racecourses on which many famous classic races are run. The horse racing industry has had a substantial impact on the surrounding countryside with the needs of horses dominating the open spaces.

The trail starts at the old red brick Newmarket Station (1), built in 1902 to replace the original Chesterford to Newmarket Railway station and terminus of 1848. The new station was built south of the old one to handle the increasing numbers of racegoers arriving in the town from the ever expanding railway system. At one time there were two restaurants to cater for passengers, one on either side of the track because the county boundary with Cambridge runs between the platforms. The station and forecourt are no longer in use for railway purposes but have been incorporated into the horse racing industry's infrastructure.

Turn right down Station Approach, as you walk down into the town Tattersalls (2) can be seen across the valley on the left, particularly the Fox Rotunda and Triumphal Arch, features that were moved from London. Turn left along The Avenue, a road constructed at the turn of the century as a more direct route to the station. Just before reaching the High Street turn left up a private road, a short way up the hill to Gibsons Saddlers (3), suppliers of jockey silks to the Royal Family.

Return to The Avenue and turn left past the picturesque Godolphin House and Scotch Tea Rooms (4) on the left, just before the junction. Turn right along the main street, passing the White Hart Hotel (5), the original coaching inn of Newmarket at which up to 20 coaches a day stopped in the 19th century. Continue on past the imposing Jockey Club building (6) and the National Horse Racing Museum (7).

Turn right into Kingston Passage (8), an area that once saw the original palace of James I who first started the improvement of the small market town into the centre of world horse racing of today. Continue through the passage to emerge by All Saints Church (9). Turn left and at the junction with All Saints Road cross to continue along Palace Street to the Palace House Mansion and Newmarket's Tourist Information Centre (10), linked to the original palace of King Charles II. Walk up the street past Nell Gwynne's House (11) on the right to reach the Rutland Arms Hotel at the corner (12).

Turn right along High Street and right again into Rous Road to reach Old Station Road, an area of mixed architecture. Turn right to the junction with Vicarage Road and the Rous Memorial Cottages (13), built in 1878 in memory of Admiral Rous, a prominent member of the Jockey Club. On the other side of the road are 18th century training stables attached to Wroughton House (14), and Cleveland House (15), built in 1820 by Lord Darlington for his jockey.

Walk on to the Machel Place Stables (16) on the right where there is a fine view up the heath and Warren Hill. Continue on as far as a red Victorian Post Box (17) in a brick wall on the right. This is directly above the railway tunnel under The Gallops, the entrance can be viewed by walking down the path to the left. Return back down Old Station Road and turn right through an alley between Nos. 13 and 15 to Sackville Street. Cross to the Moulton Road, opposite the farrier Curtis and Sons (18). Turn right to Heath House and the stables beyond, by glancing through the yard entrance you will see a creeper covered building in the centre (19). This is Fred Archer's sweatbox, used by the world's most successful jockey to keep his weight down.

Beyond the stables there is another fine view over the heath and The Gallops. You can extend the trail by walking the ³/₄ mile to the lay-by at the top of Warren Hill (20), either on the roadside verge or, if after 1 pm, over the The Gallops that are open to the public in the afternoons once the horses have been exercised. The area at the top of The Gallops was known as Kings Chair, a place where Charles II would watch the horses being trained from his shelter.

Return down Moulton Road to the clock tower (21), commemorating Queen Victoria's jubilee in 1887. Continue down the High Street on the right (north) side and turn right into the pedestrianised Market Street to the Bushel pub (22). In the cellar are traces of a cockpit where cockfighting took place in the 17th century. Continue out to the northern corner of Market Place and turn left into Rowley Drive, noting the segregated horse walk between the pavement and road. Bear off left on the path at the green, past the 15th century St. Mary's Church (23), and on along Fitzroy Street past the King Edward VII Memorial Gardens (24).

Just before the junction with Black Bear Lane is a tall undistinguished building that houses a Real Tennis Court (25), the original game that led to the modern version that we know today. Turn left along Black Bear Lane past the Fitzroy Stables and out to the High Street. Turn right up the hill passing the creeper covered former Queensbury Lodge Stables (26), the second oldest stables in Newmarket.

Continue on to the Cooper Memorial (27), a drinking fountain and horse trough at the junction with Birdcage Walk. Walk up Birdcage Walk as far as the first junction and turn left along Hamilton Road with a view over the hedge of the racecourse (28). Cross the Cambridge Road and turn left along the flint cemetery wall to an entrance gate. The cemetery was first opened in 1840 and contains the graves of many notable, owners, trainers and jockeys including that of Fred Archer (29). Follow the path left towards the Chapel and look for the tall white cross with a brass information plate against the hedge, adjacent to the Cambridge Road. Continue on down to the main entrance onto the Dullingham Road and on down the High Street.

Queensbury House (30) on the right is a fine Edwardian structure that has housed a number of royal visitors. Continue on along The Terrace (31), a raised section of pavement where you will find the headquarters of Tattersalls and No. 121, once the home of Lord Lonsdale of boxing fame. Turn right into The Avenue and retrace your steps to return to the start of the walk at the station.

Fact File

Location: Newmarket is 13 miles west of Bury St. Edmunds and 13 miles east of Cambridge
Start: Newmarket Station, Ordnance Survey map reference TL 644633
Length: 2 miles (can be extended)
Conditions: Road and roadside footway or grass on the walk extension

How to get there:–
Public Transport: For details telephone Suffolk County Council's Public Transport Information TraveLine – 08459 583358 or Anglia Rail – 08700 402020
By Road: From Ipswich west on A14 or from Cambridge east on A14
Refreshments: A wide range of shops, pubs, restaurants and takeaways in the town
Public Toilets: High Street and Cemetery
Map: Ordnance Survey Explorer sheet 210 Newmarket and Haverhill
Reference: Newmarket Town Trail by Forest Heath District Council
Information: Newmarket Tourist Information Centre – open Monday to Friday

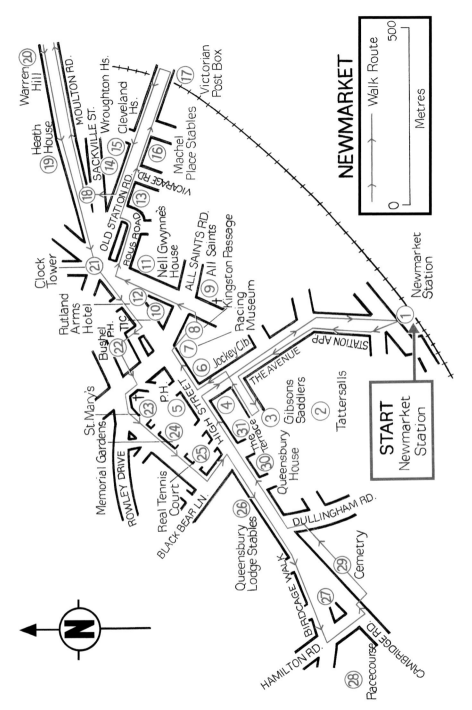

NEWMARKET

Walk Route

Metres

0   500

START
Newmarket
Station

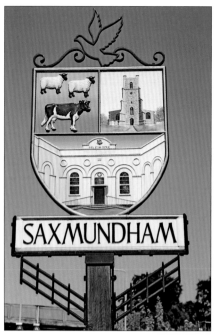

Town sign

Font in parish church

Monk's Cottages

16. Saxmundham

Saxmundham derives its name from the Saxon and Old English Seaxmund's homestead, the earliest record of the name is in the Domesday Survey which mentions three churches. The small market town stands on the River Fromus, a tributary of the River Alde, on the old A12 coaching road from London to Great Yarmouth and on the East Suffolk Railway line from Ipswich to Lowestoft.

The town trail starts at the railway station, opened in 1859 and an important point on the East Suffolk Railway for it is from this signal box that that the whole of the line is controlled. Apart from the platforms, the station building is no longer used for railway purposes, but in times past this was the junction for the Leiston and Aldeburgh branch line where holiday-makers from London made their way to the coast. The branch line closed for passengers in 1966 and now only serves the power stations at Sizewell.

Across the road is the Railway Inn (1) still providing refreshment for travellers; turn right across the tracks into Albion Street and note the railway cottages (2) on the right, with a carriageway arch at the centre. Opposite is the former old red brick Victorian police station (3) that has retained its lock-up, although it is now a private house.

Walk to the top of the street to the junction with Rendham Road and the brick base of the windmill (4) that stood here until 1907. The mill was built of wood and was extended above the height of the surrounding buildings, reputed to have been one of the tallest in Suffolk. Return to Albion Street and take the path at the side of No. 50, the local water pump stood on the right at the bottom of the steps down to Mill Road. Turn left down the road and across the railway to Chantry Road, passing the 18th century timber framed Chantry Cottages (5) on the right and Chantry House (6) on the corner.

Turn right along South Entrance noting the 3 storey 19th century house (7) built in yellow Suffolk brick and the 17th century timber framed 3 storey cottages nearby. The garage stands on the site of the first garage to be built in Saxmundham and once boasted the only petrol pump for miles around. Monks Cottages (8) on the right are some of the town's oldest dwellings and can be identified by the chequered pargetting, simulating the original 17th century style of decoration.

The last house on the right was once the home of William Bright the artist and for several years was occupied by the headquarters of Suffolk Wildlife Trust. Cross the road here and note Crown Cottage (9) with its traditional Suffolk bay window, Tudor beam and 16 inch thick front wall. Return to the crossroads and turn right into Church Street, walking over the bridge across the River Fromus and up the tree lined path to the parish Church of St. John the Baptist (10).

The church is built on a prominence overlooking the town and is thought to have been built on the site of a Saxon church, it contains portions dating from 1250. Inside is a carved stone font bearing effigies of the Woodwoses, or Wild Men of the Woods, the mystical men of Suffolk, and is surmonted by a wooden font cover bearing a figure of St. John the Baptist. Return to the road and turn right up Church Hill to the thatched cottages (11) on the right. These were built in 1836 as a single storey church school, a second floor library and reading room were added 40 years later. They have since been converted into a row of cottages.

Return down the hill and across the river, the area of Somerfields on the right (12) is the site of the town's old livestock market, granted by charter in 1272 by King Edward I to John de Ramsey, Lord of the Manor, eventually closing in 1987. Continue on to the traffic lights at the crossroads and turn right into the High Street, a conservation area containing many Tudor buildings with Victorian facades.

Particularly note the 17th century White Hart Inn (13) sporting 19th century chimneystacks and the Market Hall (14), built as a Corn Exchange in 1846 and given to the town by the Long family who have their coat of arms above the door. The Bell Inn (15) was rebuilt in 1842 on the site of a former inn and was a regular stop for the mail and stagecoaches that regularly ran the route from London to Yarmouth.

Walk on past the crinkle crankle wall on the left and see the town sign at the junction with Street Farm Road, almost opposite the Saxmundham Museum. After the railway bridge in North Entrance there are a number of fine houses to be seen. Walk on as far as Lambsale Meadow (16) and the new surgery complex that stands on the site of the former Lamb Sale and Hirings Fair that was once held here by the riverside.

Return back to the town under the railway bridge and turn right into the Market Place, an area of two parallel streets and the venue of the town's street markets for centuries. On the left are a number of cottages that have been converted from the old 16th century Angel Inn (17) that once faced the High Street and contained a cobbled yard, stables and pumped horse trough to serve the needs of travellers arriving along the A12.

At the end of the Market Place turn right into Station Approach past the front of Old Bank House (18), Saxmundham's first bank built by Gurneys in the 18th century. Walk up Station Approach to complete your walk and return to the start of the trail at the station.

Fact File

Location: Saxmundham is 23 miles north east of Ipswich and 22 miles south west of Lowestoft
Start: Saxmundham Station, Ordnance Survey map reference TM 385631
Length: $2^{1}/_{2}$ miles
Conditions: Surfaced footway and road, no stiles or gates

How to get there:–
Public Transport: For details telephone Suffolk County Council's Public Transport
 Information TraveLine – 08459 583358 or Anglia Railways – 08700 402020
By Road: From Ipswich via A1214 and A12 north, turn off on Saxmundham by-pass
Car parking: Market Place and Church Street
Refreshments: A wide range of shops, pubs, restaurants and takeaways in the town
Public Toilets: Market Place car park
Map: Ordnance Survey Explorer sheet 212 Woodbridge and Saxmundham
Reference: Draft trail leaflet by Saxmundham and District Local History Society
Information: Saxmundham Museum, 49 High Street and Crisp's Newsagents, 27 High Street

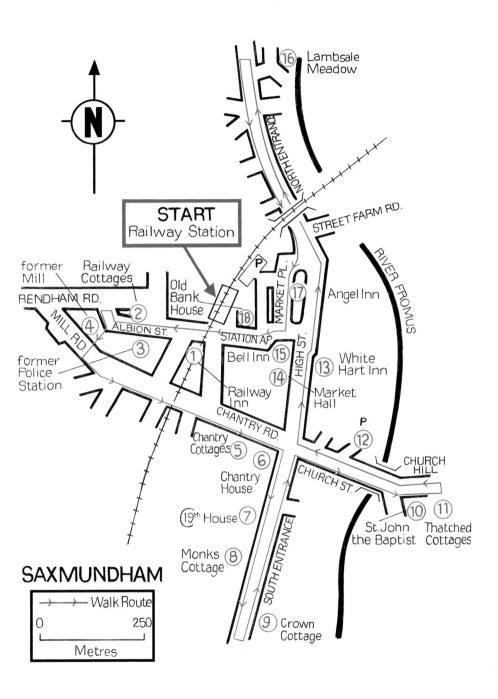

SAXMUNDHAM

Walk Route

0   250

Metres

The Southwold Museum

South Green

17. Southwold

Southwold is virtually an island surrounded by the river Blyth to the south west, Buss Creek to the north west and the North Sea to the east, there is only one road into town over Mights Bridge. The distinctive charm of Southwold stems from the haphazard layout and differing architectural designs, laced with distinctive little greens that were left unbuilt after a disastrous fire in 1659. The Town is dominated by its distinctive lighthouse and its chief glory, the medieval church of St. Edmund the Martyr and of course the closeness of the sea.

The town trail starts from the Market Place (1) where the Town Hall stands solidly next to the Swan Inn, the town's principal inn from at least the 17th century. In the centre is the town pump, standing on the site of the former Market Cross, demolished in 1809. The greengrocer's shop on the corner was the site of the Town Gaol, abandoned in 1835.

Across the road, Bank House, now Lloyds Bank, was built in 1716 for the Thompsons, one of the town's leading merchants. Turn right into Mill Lane, this once lead to the Town Mill on the Common. On the right are the Adnams Brewery stables (2), housing the horses that pull the traditional brewers dray, delivering ale from the brewery to the local hostelries around the town. Further down the lane is the former Methodist Chapel (3) with arched windows and sundial, built in 1799 and used until 1835.

At the end of Mill Lane take time to view the Common (4), extending down to the River Blyth and bequeathed to the Borough by William Godyll in 1509. Turn left along Gardner Road and left again into Park Lane. There are a variety of interesting houses and buildings here, particularly the former School of Industrial Art (5), built in 1894 to provide free teaching for local men.

After emerging at South Green turn right and follow the building line down Constitution Hill (6) to Ferry Road. This area was developed towards the end of the 18th century by the gentry seeking fashionable watering places to build their fine houses and enjoy the benefits of seaside holidays. Continue along the footway along Ferry Road, crossing to a tarmac footpath opposite the public toilets and leading up to Gun Hill (7).

The first building we come across is The Casino, built by James Thompson as a reading room in 1800 and now an RNLI museum. On the top of the hill stands a fine row of 6 muzzle-loading 18 pounder guns, cast during the reign of Elizabeth I and presented to the town in the reign of George II. Continue along the cliff top path and down to the promenade for a few metres before climbing again to the cliff top path to South Green. On the left you will pass a terrace of fine houses (8), built about 1829, before reaching the end of East Street.

Turn left down the street to the Lord Nelson pub (9), dating from just after the Battle of Trafalgar and a popular place to stop for refreshments. Return to the cliff top and the Sailors Reading Room (10) on the corner, built in 1864 as memorial to Capt. Rayley RN. Its purpose was to educate the wayward fishermen not to go to sea on Sundays and not to get drunk on any day of the week. Inside you will find items of nautical interest such as figureheads, old prints and nautical history.

Continue along the cliff top, passing East Green and on to St. James Green (11) where there is a 2 gun battery of 18th century cannon. Behind is a good view of the white lighthouse, built in 1890, it is not only a mariner's beacon but has become a landmark that identifies Southwold. Continue along the cliff top path, parallel to North Parade lined with later Victorian houses that extended the town northwards, heading down to the pier (12). The original pier was approximately 810 ft. long and completed in 1900 to enable "Belle" steamships to bring holidaymakers from Southend. The T head was swept away in a violent storm in 1934 with further damage during the last war. Although repaired in 1948, the weakened structure was struck by severe storms in 1955 and 1979, reducing the length to only reach the water's edge. Work began in 1999 to rebuild the pier and it was re-opened in July 2001.

Turn left up Pier Avenue, lined with the houses of a more recent extension to the town, bringing a range of 20th century designs to Southwold's architecture. At the mini roundabout on Station Road are the town's police and fire stations (13), standing on the site of the terminus of the former Southwold to Halesworth railway. Built in 1879 with a gauge of only 3 ft., the railway linked the town with Halesworth and the main line to Ipswich until it closed in 1929 and road transport became more popular.

Turn left up Station Road and then left again on Field Stile Road to North Green, taking the path through the gate and across the grass to the church (14). The splendid 15th century church of St. Edmund and its 100 foot tower stands on the site of a former church built in 1202 and destroyed by fire. Although fire again swept through the town in 1659 the church miraculously was the only building saved. Two particular items of note are a 15th century pulpit and a wooden Jack O' the Clock man striking a bell at the start of services.

Exit from the churchyard into Bartholomew Green, bearing to the right of the war memorial to reach the Museum (15). Housed in a small building with a Dutch shaped gable, the museum houses a variety of exhibits reflecting the history of Southwold and surrounding area. Continue along Victoria Street to the High Street and the town sign on the corner, opposite the town's Post Office (16), dating from 1895.

Turn left along the High Street, on the left is Sutherland House (17), probably dating from 1495, its current name was given to it in about 1800 by Dr. John Sutherland, a surgeon of marines. Further along on the right, set back between curved walls is Manor House (18), built around 1753 and home in the past to several of the town's prominent citizens.

A little further along is Old Bank House (19), now housing the Tourist Information Centre, and opposite, the Crown Hotel. This dates from around 1750 when it was the King's Head; it changed to the Crown in 1829. Just before reaching the end of the walk at Market Place (1), note on the right Buckenham House (20), also known as the Old Vicarage, it was the property of Richard Buckenham in 1571.

Fact File

Location: Southwold is 31 miles north east of Ipswich, 11 miles south of Lowestoft
Start: Southwold Market Place Ordnance Survey map reference TM 508760
Length: 2^1/$_2$ miles
Conditions: Town footways and road, no steps or stiles

How to get there:—
Public Transport: For details telephone Suffolk County Council's Public Transport Information TraveLine – 08459 583358
Road Route: From Ipswich north on A12 and A1095 to Southwold
Car Parking: Free at Common car parks or pay and display at Pier and other car parks
Refreshments: Wide range of facilities for all tastes throughout the town
Public Toilets: Pier, Victoria Street and Promenade
Map: Ordnance Survey Explorer sheet 231 Southwold and Bungay
Reference: Discovering Southwold by Southwold and Reydon Society and Suffolk Preservation Society
Information: Southwold Tourist Information Centre – open daily all year

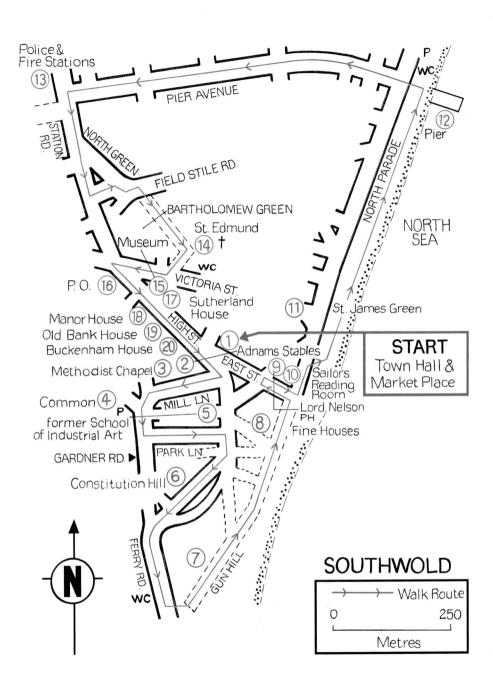

Police &
Fire Stations
⑬

STATION RD.

PIER AVENUE

NORTH GREEN

FIELD STILE RD.

BARTHOLOMEW GREEN

St. Edmund ✝
⑭

Museum

WC

P.O. ⑯
⑮

VICTORIA ST.
⑰ Sutherland
House

Manor House ⑱
Old Bank House ⑲
Buckenham House ⑳
Methodist Chapel ③ ②

HIGH ST.

EAST ST.

Adnams Stables
①

⑪ St. James Green

⑨
⑩ Sailors
Reading
Room

Common ④
P

former School
of Industrial Art

MILL LN.
⑤

⑧

Lord Nelson
PH
Fine Houses

GARDNER RD. ▶

PARK LN.

Constitution Hill ⑥

FERRY RD.

WC

⑦

GUN HILL

N

P
WC

⑫
Pier

NORTH PARADE

NORTH
SEA

START
Town Hall &
Market Place

SOUTHWOLD

→ Walk Route

0   250

Metres

Reproduced from Ordnance Survey mapping on behalf of The Controller of Her Majesty's Stationery Office
© Crown Copyright. Licence Number AL100037826.

79

Stowmarket Station

Maltings on the River Gipping

18. Stowmarket

The ancient town of Stowmarket lies just about in the centre of Suffolk, although its origins are impossible to date. Its name has pre-Saxon roots, Stowe meaning meeting place, and evidence of Roman settlement has been found in the area. Stowe was the name of the administrating hundred and the word market had been added by 1253. The town particularly came to prominence during the 19th century when trading access to and from Ipswich was opened up with the canalisation of the River Gipping and later the arrival of the railway.

The town trail starts from the Museum of East Anglian Life (1) situated close to the centre of the town. The museum covers about 70 acres and includes a number of historic buildings that have been moved from other parts of the region. Next to the museum entrance note the black weather boarded tithe barn with red pantile roof that dates back to the 14th century when it was built by the Priory of St. Osyth that held the manor of Stowmarket.

Walk down the footpath to the right of the supermarket, past the Tourist Information Centre (2) to Crowe Street. Continue left into the Market Place (3) where there is an array of imposing buildings, including bank premises and 18th and 19th century shops. Turn left and walk up to the traffic lights at the junction of Tavern Street and Bury Street (4), the point where two of Suffolk's old medieval roads crossed. Return to the Market Place and turn left into the Buttermarket (5) with the former Rose Inn at the end on the right. The town once had over 40 inns but less than 10 remain open today.

Continue on past the church of St. Peter and St. Mary (6), mainly 14th century and of large proportions, demonstrating the wealth of the area in medieval times. The unusual dedication results from there having been two churches within the churchyard, St. Mary's was demolished in 1544. The church had a new spire in 1993 to replace previous structures that had been destroyed by storm and dismantled because of decay, it is unusual in that it has a gallery within its height. The south side of the churchyard is bounded by a terrace of cottages built of white Suffolk bricks and timber framed buildings known as Bull's Row. Turn left at the end of the church and out onto Station Road East, opposite a raised section of pavement known as a Carnser. The white brick building opposite was once the Stevens Brewery (7), in 1840 a 330 feet deep well was sunk which eventually became the town's water supply until the 1970s.

Turn right down to Gipping Way, the large red and white brick building on the corner is Lynton House (8), a 17th century building refaced in the 19th century and was the town house of the Tyrell family of Gipping. Cross Gipping Way and turn left before bearing right down the path to Stowupland Street (9), now truncated by the new road. This was the medieval heart of the town and in the centre of the industrial revolution.

Straight ahead is the kiln roof of the Union Maltings, the last open floor maltings to operate in the town. At the height of the industry there were over 50 maltings of this type in the town, taking advantage of the improved access provided by the canalised river. Follow the road round to the right and then turn left into Union Street East to the Royal William pub (10) at the end. Turn right to reach the Methodist Chapel (11), built of Suffolk white bricks in 1836, at the junction of Regent Street and Bond Street.

Turn right to Stowupland Street and then left to the bridge (12) over the river. There was once a ford at this point and also the head of the navigation as can be seen in the contrasting widths of the river either side of the bridge. Turn right along the river path, this area was known as Navigation Wharf with maltings, warehouses and timber yards constructed on both side of the river. The navigation to Ipswich was opened in 1793, is 17 miles long and required the construction of 15 locks, by 1800 there were 40 barges in use.

At the Station Road bridge (13) turn left to the station (14). This fine structure in red brick was designed by Fredrick Barnes and completed in 1849. It is recorded that the local townspeople donated £1000 towards the costs in order that they had a station worthy of the town. Return to the river, noting the former maltings on the left, now listed buildings and put to a new use. Turn left along the river path once again, by the steps there is an information board about the river and the Gipping Valley River Path.

Walk along the old towpath and cross the river via the footbridge just before the weir (15), following the path out to Gipping Way. Cross to the right and around the former Scout Hut (16) (corrugated iron roof), to reach a path at the side of No. 51. Walk into the grounds of the Old Vicarage continuing straight on and then left around the back of the building and into the front garden (17). Now owned by Stowmarket Town Council the house was once the home of Dr. Thomas Young, a close friend of John Milton. The Mulberry tree in the front lawn is reputed to have been planted by Milton on one of his visits. Note also the curious bay window on the end of the ballroom, now the Town Council's Meeting Chamber.

Turn right along Milton Road to Ipswich Street and then right through the town. Of particular note on the right is the Old Fox Yard (18), once a coaching Inn and now a small shopping complex. Just before reaching the Market Place turn left along Marriots Walk (19) to Camping Land (20), an open area of grass and trees. This area was reputed to be where the ancient game of camp or campen, a rough game of football was played, parish against parish until the end of the 18th century.

Turn right along the footpath at the edge of the grass to the gates of Abbotts Hall on the left (21), the old manor house, continuing straight on to return to the start at the museum.

Fact File

Location: Stowmarket is 12 miles north west of Ipswich and 12 miles southeast of Bury St Edmunds
Start: Museum of East Anglian Life, Ordnance Survey map reference TM 047585
Length: Approximately 1^1/$_2$ miles
Conditions: Town paths and road, steps at river can be avoided

How to get there:–
Public transport: For details telephone Suffolk County Council's Public Transport Information TraveLine – 08459 583358 or Anglia Railways – 08700 402020
By Road: A14 from Ipswich or Bury St. Edmunds then A1120, follow signs for Museum of East Anglian Life
Car Parking: Illife Way near the Museum of East Anglian Life and others
Refreshments: A wide range of facilities in the town
Public Toilets: Off the Illife Way car park
Map: Ordnance Survey Explorer sheet 211 Bury St Edmunds and Stowmarket
Reference: A Walk Around Stowmarket published by Stowmarket Town Council
Information: Mid Suffolk Tourist Information Centre, Stowmarket – open all year Monday to Saturday

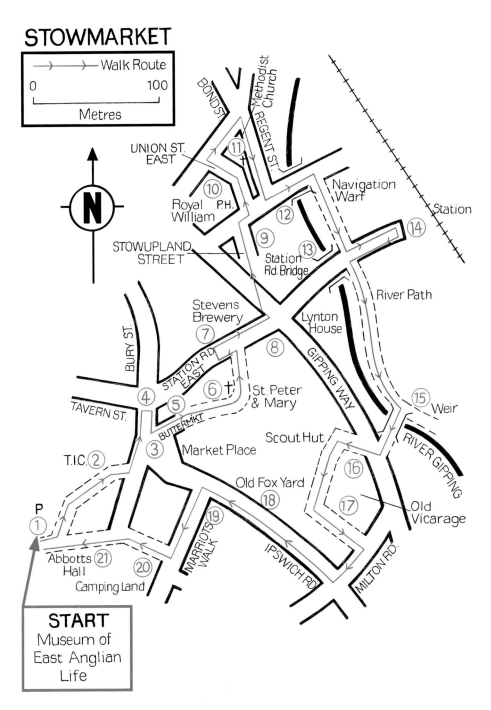

Gainsborough's House

Old house on Mill Hill

19. Sudbury

Sudbury takes its name from the Old English 'suth' and 'burg' meaning a southern fortified settlement and stands on high ground in a loop of the River Stour, similar to Bungay on the River Waveney. From medieval prosperity the town continued to expand due to the influence of the Flemish weavers and the wool trade of the area. In 1705 the creation of the navigation along the River Stour from Manningtree provided the means to rapidly transport the output until it closed in 1916. The railway came to the area in 1849 when the first section of the Stour Valley Railway, from its junction with the London to Colchester main line, opened.

The town's most famous son was the painter Thomas Gainsborough, born in his parent's house in Gainsborough Street (formerly Sepulchre Street) in 1727, he died in 1788 and is buried at Kew. The Gainsborough family came from Lincolnshire when the artist's grand-father was apprenticed to a local clothier, eventually creating his own business and becoming involved in town affairs. The town trail explores the areas of Sudbury that the artist Thomas Gainsborough would have known and fittingly ends at the Gainsborough House Museum.

The walk starts from Gainsborough's statue by Sir Bertram Mackennel, at the top of Market Hill (1), with a fine backdrop provided by the redundant St. Peter's church. Walk to the left of the church into Old Market Place and turn left into North Street. On the north east corner is a group of buildings (2) that were owned by the Dupont's, a family that Gainsborough's sister had married into. Further along on the north side of North Street is the preserved red brick gateway (3) to an 18th century charity school, built on the site of Sudbury Manor and now a car park. Continue along North Street, noting No. 63 (4), one of the few remaining red brick buildings that would have lined this street in Gainsborough's day.

Turn left into New Street, walking down between the Victorian houses towards St. Gregory's church. Cross the busy road and enter the churchyard through the east gate. Just before reaching the south door note the tomb of George Fulcher on the right, five times mayor of Sudbury. The church contains a 15th century font cover that survived the puritan vandalism of William Dowsing in 1643. Leave the churchyard by the south gate and continue straight on to the junction with Walnuttree Lane.

Turn right down the hill past the former workhouse, now a hospital and, where the lane bears left, note the white building on the corner (5). This is now part of the Mill Hotel but was Ann Gainsborough's house, widow of the artist's elder brother Robert. Continue on down the lane past the Mill Hotel (6) and turn left up Mill Hill into Stour Street for a few metres. This section of road (7) contains a variety of 15th, 16th, 17th, 18th and 19th (flint) buildings.

Return down Mill Hill pausing to look at the typical Suffolk pink house on the right (8) one of the oldest surviving homesteads in Sudbury and on the left in Cross Street, a superb timber framed building (9) that was used for town meetings in the 15th century. Just before reaching the junction with Church Street, on the right you will find the former White Hart pub (10) with etched glass windows, known to Gainsborough as the Kings Arms.

Walk out of the town over the River Stour across the Ballingdon Bridge (11) and under the iron bridge of the former railway. Although the track now ends at Sudbury, this was once a through route to Cambridge. Opened in 1849, it finally closed in 1967. The track bed is now a popular country walk and, together with the meadows of the Town's Common Lands, bring the countryside close to the centre of the town.

Pause at Ballingdon House (12), home of Emily Gainsborough, Thomas's great-granddaughter. Continue on along the street (13), the wide pavements here would once have been grassed over and lined with market stalls. At the end of Ballingdon Street, at the crossroads, stands the King's Head pub (14), the last of many alehouses that once abounded in this area.

Return to the town across the Ballingdon Bridge and turn right into Church Street, noting the Old Bull Inn (15), a haunt of the artist's brother John. He was known as 'Scheming Jack' because of his hair-brained inventions. Continue on past All Saints Church, the third of Sudbury's main churches, and then past the Baptist Church, to turn right into Friars Street. On the corner stands a fine 18th century building (16) with shop fronts that have been preserved and further along the Ship and Star (17) once part of a Dominican Priory. Standing back on the left opposite the Priory Gatehouse is a range of buildings (18) once occupied by Gainsborough's sister Susan where she set up as a milliner. Her husband Richard Gardiner was at one time the town's Postmaster and this was known as Post Office Square. After passing the cricket ground, and a little further up the street, on the right is a prominent 18th century timber framed building (19) once occupied by the artist's clothier uncle Thomas. Finally on the left is the Anchor (20), once part of the White Hart Inn, one of a number of alehouses that were in this street.

At the Midland (HSBC) Bank (21) on the corner, look up the hill to the Black Boy Hotel (22), standing on the site of The Bull where bulls were publicly baited. Turn left along Gainsborough Street past Burkitts Lane, named after the Birkitt family, a prominent and wealthy local business family, much admired by the Gainsborough's. Their red brick family house (23) stands on the left corner of the lane facing onto Gainsborough Street.

Finally we come to Gainsborough's House (24), the family home, now run by a private charitable trust and exhibiting more of his work than any other gallery in the world. The house is usually open to the public every day and is a fine culmination to the walk, a visit is essential if you wish to study the local links with Gainsborough.

Fact File

Location: Sudbury is 18 miles west of Ipswich and 16 miles south of Bury St. Edmunds
Start: Market Hill, Ordnance Survey map reference TL974413
Length: 2 miles
Conditions: Roadside footway throughout

How to get there:—
Public Transport: For details telephone Suffolk County Council's Public Transport Information TraveLine – 08459 583358 or rail information – 08457 484950
Road Route: From Ipswich on A1071 and A134, or from Bury St. Edmunds south on A134
Car Parking: Station Road/Great Eastern Road and others
Refreshments: A wide range of facilities available in the town
Public Toilets: In town centre
Map: Ordnance Survey Explorer sheet 196 Sudbury, Hadleigh and Dedham Vale
Reference: Gainsborough's Sudbury by Edith Freeman, David Tyler and Angela Lewis Johnson, available for £3.00 from the T.I.C. and local bookshops
Information: Sudbury Tourist Information Centre – open daily and Gainsborough's House open daily except Mondays, Good Friday and between Christmas and New Year

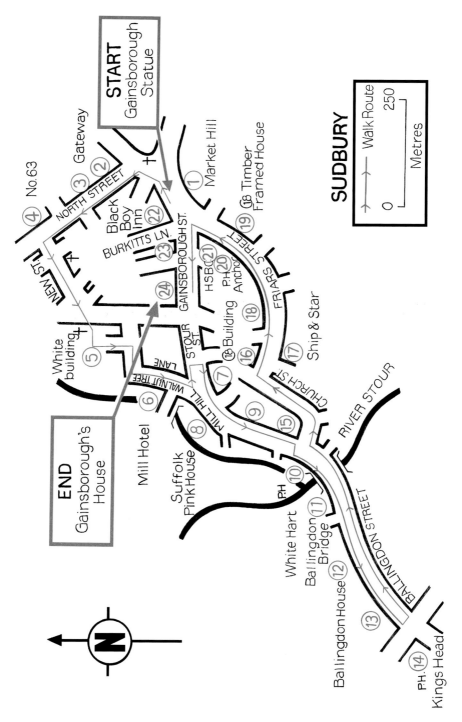

SUDBURY

→ Walk Route

0   250

Metres

START
Gainsborough
Statue

END
Gainsborough's
House

N

① Market Hill
② Gateway
③ No.63
④ No.63
⑤ White building
⑥
⑦
⑧
⑨
⑩
⑪ Ballingdon Bridge
⑫ Ballingdon House
⑬
⑭ Kings Head
⑮
⑯
⑰ Ship & Star
⑱
⑲
⑳ HSBC
㉑
㉒ Black Boy Inn
㉓
㉔
⑱ Timber Framed House
⑱ Building

NORTH STREET
NEW ST.
BURKITTS LN.
GAINSBOROUGH ST.
STOUR ST.
FRIARS STREET
WALNUT TREE LANE
MILL HILL
CHURCH ST.
BALLINGDON STREET
RIVER STOUR

Mill Hotel
Suffolk Pink House
White Hart
P.H.
Anchor
P.H.

Harbour and Tide Mill

Shire Hall

20. Woodbridge

The town seems to take its name from a bridge that may have once straddled the river but no details of the structure can be found. The name may either mean a wooden bridge or a bridge near a wood, an alternative explanation is that the name derives from Woden's town. The situation of the market town and port on the estuary of the River Deben makes it a favourite place for yachtsmen and visitors, its early medieval prosperity was based on the shipbuilding and local trade that developed various sea-faring activities. History about the town can be found in the Woodbridge Museum, situated on Market Hill on the walk route.

The town trail starts from the railway station (1), opened in 1859 when the first trains from Ipswich were able to travel north after difficulties building the track bed at Playford. Although the first engine to reach Woodbridge came from the north, it wasn't until 3rd March 1859 that a train was able to travel the route from Ipswich. The line finally opened for business on 1st June 1859, even though there were no timetables available at Woodbridge.

From the station car park cross the railway on the pedestrian bridge, adjacent to the Riverside Theatre, to reach the quay. From the vantage point of the bridge view the harbour area and look across the river to Sutton Hoo on the far bank where the Saxon burial ship of King Radwald was discovered during excavations between 1936 and 1939. A ferry once plied the river, taking passengers to the small landing stage on the other side. Turn left and follow the harbour wall around Ferry Quay and right along Tide Mill Way. The Tide Mill (2) is one of the earliest tide mills to be recorded in Britain and was the last working example in the country. The present building dates from 1793 and was restored and opened to the public in 1975. Now completed, the mill operates from the reduced tidal pool at the rear and, depending on the tides, you can see the mill wheel turning the machinery inside.

Return along Tide Mill Way and across the railway to Quay Side, turn right along the roadside footway to Brook Street on the left. Turn up towards the town between the picturesque cottages and old warehouses that line the street to the Thoroughfare (3), once the main road from Ipswich to Lowestoft. This is also the main shopping area of the town and well worth a bit of further investigation.

Cross to New Street (new in 1550), and walk up past the library and St Johns Hill. In the upper section of New Street note Bridewell (4), the former jail, one of the few exposed timber framed buildings in Woodbridge with pegged joints, and the Olde Bell and Steelyard (5). The overhanging projection or steelyard was used to weigh loaded carts on their way down to the river from the market place and then empty carts on the way back, it was last operated in 1880.

Continue on to reach Market Hill, the medieval centre of Woodbridge with the picturesque Shire Hall standing in the centre. The Bull Hotel (6) on the left is an old coaching inn, John Groats, a former landlord bred horses and sold them to the King of Italy and the Viceroy of India. Beyond the courtyard is the grave of Carlow whose charity still distributes bread. Turn right up the hill, noting the building on the right with the initials EFG and date 1860–1873 over the door (7). This is where Edward Fitzgerald lived from 1860 to 1873, he translated the Rubaiyat of Omar Khayyam from Persian to English, and is buried at nearby Boulge Church.

Walk up around the Shire Hall (8), which was built by the town's main benefactor Thomas Seckford (1515–1587), to house the court sessions that were moved from Melton. This event marked the replacement of Wickham Market by Woodbridge as the regional centre. The ground floor was also once used as a corn market with arches to accommodate waggons and is now the offices of the town council. The upper floor houses the Suffolk Horse Museum, dedicated to the Suffolk Punch. The town pump (9) was provided by the Seckford Foundation and designed with stone pools to provide drinking water for horses and dogs in addition to the needs of local residents. At the top of Market Hill stands the Kings Head (10), reckoned to be the oldest building in Woodbridge and once the guildhall.

Walk down the other side of Market Hill to the Woodbridge Museum (11), a timber framed building with later Georgian brick facade, opposite Edward Fitzgerald's house. Return back to The Alley (12), a cobbled entry opposite the pump, and turn left down the worn cobble stones and steps to the church yard, opposite the main door of St. Mary's Church (13). The tower is 108 feet high, reflecting the town's former prosperity, Thomas Seckford was buried here in 1587. Turn left to the churchyard gates leading out to Church Street (14), a street with a wide variety of buildings, ages and styles. Look through the gateway on the right to the Abbey School (15), built near the site of an Augustinian Priory, demolished in 1537, the material being used to build the Abbey.

Continue down Church Street and turn right into Turn Lane. Look out for a door into the Quaker Graveyard (16) where the poet Bernard Barton is buried, next to it is the Friends Meeting House (17). Continue along the lane as it becomes an alley and emerges out on to Cumberland Street, an extension of the Thoroughfare, and also once the main road through the town. Turn left, noting the fine variety of buildings on both sides of the street, Barton's Cottage (18) on the right was described by Barton as 'My little nutshell of a house'. Note also Marston House and Gordon House (19) on the left which were named after officers who occupied them during the Napoleonic wars when Woodbridge was a garrison town.

At Cross Corner note the Crown Hotel (20) that is an old coaching inn and turn right into Quay Street. As you walk towards the harbour look out for the old kiln and chapel (21) on the left and opposite, the white painted Old Customs House. Continue on down to Station Road and cross via the pedestrian crossing to the start of the trail in the station car park.

Fact File

Location: Woodbridge is 8 miles north east of Ipswich and 43 miles south west of Lowestoft
Start: Woodbridge Railway Station, Ordnance Survey map reference TM 273487
Length: 1 mile
Conditions: Some steps but easy walking

How to get there:–

Public Transport: For details telephone Suffolk County Council's Public Transport Information TraveLine – 08459 583358 or Anglia Railways – 08700 402020
By Road: A12 from Ipswich or Lowestoft, follow signs for the railway station
Car parking: Plenty of parking around the area of the station
Refreshments: A wide range of facilities including a cafe in the station building
Public Toilets: Several in town, look for signs
Map: Ordnance Survey Explorer sheet 197 Ipswich, Felixstowe and Harwich
Reference: Woodbridge Town Trail by the Woodbridge Museum
Information: Woodbridge Tourist Information Centre – open all year

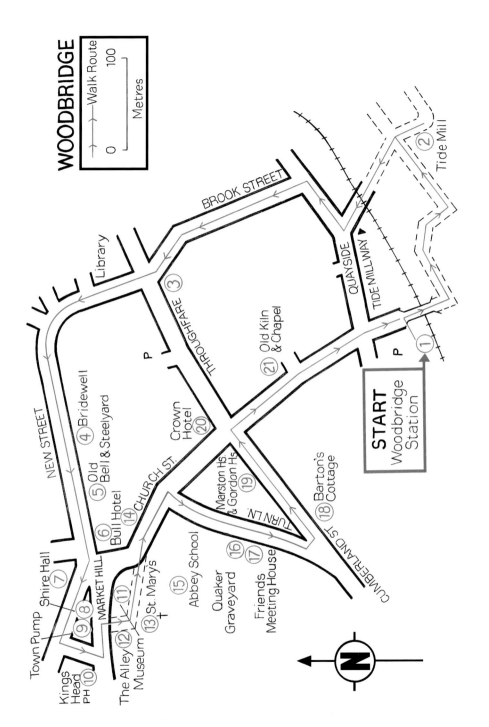

WOODBRIDGE

→ Walk Route

0   100
Metres

START
Woodbridge
Station

2 Tide Mill
1
BROOK STREET
QUAYSIDE
TIDE MILLWAY
3 THROUGHFARE
21 Old Kiln & Chapel
Library
P
4 Bridewell
5 Old Bell & Steelyard
6 Bull Hotel
20 Crown Hotel
NEW STREET
CHURCH ST.
14
7 Shire Hall
Town Pump
8
9
10 Kings Head PH
11
12 The Alley
13 Museum
St. Mary's
MARKET HILL
15 Abbey School
16 Quaker Graveyard
17 Friends Meeting House
Marston Hs & Gordon Hs
19
18 Barton's Cottage
TURN LN.
CUMBERLAND ST.
P

N

Reproduced from Ordnance Survey mapping on behalf of The Controller of Her Majesty's Stationery Office
© Crown Copyright. Licence Number AL100037826.

View from Beccles Bridge

Bury St. Edmund's Cathedral